A man and his God

A Man and his God

Denis Lane

EVANGELICAL PRESS

EVANGELICAL PRESS
16/18, High Street, Welwyn, Hertfordshire
AL6 9EQ, England

© Evangelical Press 1981

First published 1981
Second impression 1984

ISBN 0 85234 155 5

Printed by Anchor Brendon Ltd., Tiptree, Colchester, England.

Contents

1.	Faith in God	7
2.	Faith and life	17
3.	Faith and the two worlds	28
4.	Faith and famine	38
5.	Faith and family quarrels	47
6.	Faith's widening vision	62
7.	Faith and politics	70
8.	Faith looks upward and forward	79
9.	Faith under depression	91
10.	Faith and home-made solutions	99
11.	Faith and fresh experience	110
12.	Faith faces the impossible	122
13.	Faith learns to pray	130
14.	Faith finds fulfilment and performs a parable	138
15.	Faith's final test	147
16.	Faith looks for a country	158

1

Faith in God

'If only I had more faith!' 'She is a person of tremendous faith.' 'I wish I could have the faith that you do.' People often say things like these.

'Faith' has something of a magic ring about it. We feel that if only we could get hold of it, then life would be different. On the other hand, some Christians feel that faith has not come up to their expectations. They had been told that if they put their faith in Christ then everything would go well. Everything has not gone well. So, surrounded by intractable problems, they begin to wonder whether faith is so wonderful after all. Very often the problem is that we have not understood what faith, in the Christian sense, is all about in the first place. We have imparted to it a magical quality of its own that it was never meant to have. For faith is not a wand to wave over life to iron out the creases. Indeed faith, in itself, is nothing. It only becomes effective when acting as a living link between the God who made and directs the world, and the human creatures who live in it. We are going to look at the life of a man who demonstrated what faith involves, a man who faced considerable problems in his life and circumstances and yet who found through them all that God is real and God is reliable. The man's name is Abraham.

Paul tells us in his letter to the Romans that those who believe in Christ 'share the faith of Abraham'. Abraham is called in this connection the 'father of us all'. In other words, his life is more than just an example of a man who believed in God. He is rather a prototype. He is the first man in the Bible to show clearly in his life and his relationships the fundamental attitude and response that should be the mark of us all. And he is said, in the words of the Amplified New Testament, to have been 'empowered by faith'.

We must not, however, think of Abraham as an extra special kind of believer. We must not put him on a pedestal as an outstanding example of something that we can all aim at, but only few can reach. Rather, he is chosen as someone who showed in his life the basic elements that go to make up the life of faith. A specialist who is teaching medical students will show them a particular case where the symptoms of a disease are clearly evident, so that they may learn to recognize the problem in others whose symptoms are less clearly marked. Abraham is the first clinical example that occurs in the Bible of someone living by faith. Earlier in Genesis (5:24) we are told that Enoch walked with God, but we are not told how that worked out for him, so, while we admire Enoch, he does not help us very much if we want to do the same. In Abraham's case we see the life of faith, 'warts and all', and we see it, not set out in a series of propositions, but lived out in the sands of the desert and the turmoils of a family. In the end Abraham was called the 'friend of God', a title that expresses both the familiarity and closeness of the relationship that existed and the awesome nature of that relationship when a human creature could be so described. Yet Jesus Himself said to His disciples, 'You are my friends.' Faith is at the root of that relationship.

Our specialist friend is glad that he can take his students to see a clear case of the disease they are studying, but he has to go further than that. He needs to analyse the condition, to explain how the structure of the body cells is affected by it and describe what is happening in terms that his students can understand. The patient would not be too happy to think of himself in these analytical terms, but in the end he will benefit from the exercise. So we must take the living case of Abraham and analyse his faith and its contents, not to rob it of its personal significance, but in order that we might learn how we, too, may live like that.

When we start to analyse Abraham's faith, we realize first of all that *faith begins with God and His Word.* Genesis 12 begins, 'The Lord had said to Abram . . .' This eliminates right away some of our magical ideas about faith. Faith is not something that happens to us in a vacuum. It does not suddenly descend upon us out of the sky as a marvellous feeling. In fact, faith cannot exist without something and someone to whom to respond. God spoke to Abraham and he responded with belief and commitment. Without the prior word, there could have been no faith. Faith, then, does not begin with us, but with God who speaks His Word. Therefore the real value does not lie in our faith, but in the Word that has come to us and in the God who speaks it. This puts faith into perspective as something which has no value in itself, but which derives its value from the response it makes to what is already there.

In his letter to the Romans (10:14-17) Paul expounds this idea in another context: 'How, then, can they call on the one they have not believed in?' he says. People do not respond to someone unless there is something to which to respond. He then goes on to the next logical step: 'And how can they believe in the one of whom they have not heard?' Faith is not possible without something on which to base it, and if we have never heard of someone we cannot possibly respond to him. Paul then points out that someone must proclaim the message if the people are to hear, and someone must be sent by God to do the proclaiming. Without these things there can be no faith, because there is no message to which to respond. Paul's conclusion then is 'Consequently, faith comes from hearing the message, and the message is heard through the word of Christ.' Faith therefore cannot exist without a message to which to respond, and faith in God cannot exist without a word from God to which to respond.

Actually we practise faith in many people's words every day. When we stand at a bus-stop and board a bus with the right number and the right destination, we are responding to the word of the bus company that promises to take us there. We cannot see the destination any more than we can see God. We do not normally haggle with the conductor about whether he is telling the truth from the front of his bus. We certainly do not ask him to prove that he is going there before we will step on board. We are so used to the company telling the truth about the destination of their buses that we are ready to take them at their word. If there is no destination marked on the bus we may hesitate to commit ourselves and ask the conductor where he is going. Then we respond to his word. But someone, somewhere, must give us a message to which we can respond, if we are to have faith. Faith in God is different only in the sense that the stakes are higher, the consequences of lack of response are more serious and longer lasting, and the Person who speaks the word is utterly reliable.

Abraham's response of faith is more remarkable than ours, in the sense that few people before his time had heard the message of God addressed to them. We have the Word of God to the human race clearly set out for us in the pages of the Scriptures. We have centuries of revelation addressed to us there, and we have the life of Jesus Christ, the living embodiment of the message of God to men, set out in the clear light of day. Therefore, if we have a Bible, we cannot say that, unlike Abraham, we do not know what God's message to us really is. The Word is available and calls continually to men and women to think again in repentance about a way of life that leaves God right out of the picture. The Word calls them to come to Jesus Christ in trust and commitment to find forgiveness and reconciliation and new life through His death upon the cross and the resurrection and ascension that followed it.

Yet, just at this point, we need to recognize the second element in saving faith, which lies in *the effectual and personal call of God through His Word addressed to the believer*. Abraham did not just hear words. He was conscious that those words were addressed to him personally. He was face to face with God and God was inviting him to respond to a call to walk with Him and relate to Him. It was as though there was no one else there. Every believer knows this experience. Paul describes his own sense of it in Galatians 1:13-16. He had been a very religious man and really thought that it was right to try to destroy the church of God. He was extremely zealous, indeed more so than his contemporaries. Then, he says, 'God, who set me apart from birth and called me by his grace, was pleased to reveal his Son in me.' There came a time in his life when God broke in and called him to change his way and commit himself to Jesus Christ.

Matthew knew this kind of call when Jesus passed his office one day and said, 'Follow me.' Peter and Andrew knew it, too, when Jesus said to them as they were fishing, 'Come, follow me, and I will make you fishers of men' (Matthew 4:19). The Holy Spirit of God comes to men and women today with this conviction that God is speaking personally to them and, when He comes, the attraction of God's grace and love becomes irresistible and they respond with the commitment of their lives to Him. Faith, then, is something warm and living. The written Word becomes the living Word to our souls. The hymn-writer expressed it in these terms:

Heaven above is softer blue,
Earth around is deeper green,
Something lives in every hue,
Christless eyes have never seen.

Faith of this kind is as different from cold orthodoxy as is chalk from cheese. And it was just this element of reality and personal relationship that kept Abraham going through the darkest of the days that lay ahead.

Someone may say at this point, 'What do I do if I have never known the Holy Spirit coming to me to make God's Word personal to my own life and experience?' The only answer I can give to that question is to seek God in and through His Word and ask Him to come to you and make the invitations of that Word real and personal to you. I cannot make it real to you, nor can any human person, for 'all who received him' and 'those who believed in his name' and who therefore have 'the right to become children of God', are born 'not of natural descent', that is, because their family believed, 'nor of human decision', that is, their own will power, 'or of a husband's will', that is, because someone else wanted it to happen. Such people are, on the contrary, 'born of God' and the initiative lies with Him (John 1:12,13). Yet, knowing His love and grace, we can have every confidence that if we seek we shall find, and if we knock it will be opened to us, and the very fact that we want to seek Him at all is a sign of His working in us already.

The third aspect of true faith in God that Abraham shows so clearly is that *faith is commitment to a Person to walk with Him in relationship*. Genesis 12:1-3 makes this plain by the frequent use of the pronouns 'I' and 'you'. Abraham is to 'leave' and to 'go' and God will 'make' him, 'bless' him and bless others through him. God called him to a new relationship and to one that made certain demands upon him and brought certain guarantees to him. The important thing for the moment, however, is to see that true faith is not the commitment of a moment, but the commencement of a relationship. Just as marriage is much more than saying, 'I will', during a ceremony, and demands constant cultivation of an ongoing relationship, so faith responds through life and not just once. This is important, for today a great emphasis is sometimes placed on 'deciding for Christ', as though that in itself would guarantee everything from then on. People can then assume that they have done all that is necessary to secure their future and little further response is called for. 'Deciding' is not a good word in any case, for it implies that unaided we make up our minds to follow Christ. It places all the initiative with us. As we have already seen, that is not the case, so a better expression would be 'responding to Christ', for He makes the first approach. Biblical faith commits us to a lasting relationship and to doing all on our part to deepen it. God can be relied upon to fulfil His part in developing the union. So when the word from

God came to Abraham, He was looking down the future to many things that would take years to complete, and He was asking Abraham to respond then and throughout his life to an ever-deepening relationship.

Someone may now be asking, 'What is the basis of the relationship with God that you are writing about? I can see that faith is a response to a message from God, but what is that message for us today? Abraham was told to get up and leave his friends and go out to another country. Obviously God does not intend us to do that. What is He asking from us?' The answers to these questions are very clearly set out in Romans 3:21–26 in the truth known as justification by faith. Paul was writing about right relationships between God and man and the basis on which they can exist. The first thing he had to do was to get rid of a wrong idea that still fills most people's minds when they think of a relationship with God. The wrong idea is that we can somehow merit God's favour and, by good deeds done since then, cancel out any quarrel He may have with our behaviour in the past and earn His favourable response. So Paul spent most of the first part of his letter showing that the chances of our meriting the favour of God are absolutely nil. Whether we are down and out in moral degradation, respectable and moral in polite society, or very religious in keeping the rules, when we come up against the absolute standards of God, we fall flat on our faces and can do nothing to remedy the situation. His conclusion therefore is that 'no-one will be declared righteous in his sight by observing the law' (Romans 3:20). No amount of doing good will be any help. In fact, 'Through the law we become conscious of sin.' When we begin to measure ourselves against God's real standards, and not against our own watered-down versions, then we sink further and further into despair at any possibility of meeting the requirements. Such teaching may not seem at first sight to be of much help, but it is necessary if we are to accept the real remedy.

The great message of the good news of God comes to people aware of their failure to achieve God's standards for their lives, bringing the announcement of acceptance into right relationship as a free gift from God. Paul describes this as 'a righteousness from God, apart from law', that is, apart from the best of human efforts. It comes wholly on God's own initiative and on a totally new basis. All men and women 'have sinned and fall short of the glory of God' (Romans 3:23) and therefore share in a common failure, but to such people God offers the prospect of being treated as though absolutely just and of receiving this new relationship, 'freely by his grace through the redemption that came by Christ Jesus'.

To many people this sounds not only too good to be true, but morally and ethically suspect. If human sin and failure count for anything, surely God, the righteous Judge, cannot turn round and offer a free pardon all round. Besides, this seems too easy. The secret lies in the words: 'through the redemption that came by Christ Jesus'. When goods are redeemed from a pawnbroker a price has to be paid for their release. The pawnbroker does not worry who pays the money, but nothing leaves his shop without the cost of release being handed over. The 'redemption that came by Christ Jesus' is the price He paid that people might be set free and counted as righteous. That price Paul further describes, in no cheap terms, as 'a sacrifice of atonement', an offering of a life freely laid down to make full satisfaction of all demands rightly made upon

another. Jesus Christ alone could pay the price for
others, for He alone had no price to pay for His own
failure. He would pay for all men, because He Himself is
God the Son and therefore of infinite value.

Therefore Paul could rightly claim that in the
sacrificial offering of the cross God was demonstrating
His justice. In the cross God was openly saying that sin is
serious and a payment must be made. Yet, at the same
time, because the payment was made by the sinless Son
of God, God could accept as cleared and justified any
who would believe that Jesus had died for them, and
relate to God on the basis of a living trust in His death
(v.26).

Despite the amazing generosity of this offer that God
still holds out to a dying world, men and women still
labour to 'make it' on their own, spurning the mighty
drama of God's saving work in Christ as too easy or too
simple. The truth is rather that to confess that we have
no means of making it on our own and to accept that we
are totally dependent upon the death of Jesus Christ on
the cross is often too humbling to our pride. 'Surely' we
feel, 'I can do something.' Only a deep sense of how
serious is our spiritual need can drive us to the truly
Christian confession of Augustus Toplady:

> Nothing in my hand I bring,
> Simply to Thy cross I cling,
> Naked come to Thee for dress,
> Helpless, look to Thee for grace,
> Vile I to the fountain fly,
> Wash me, Saviour, *or I die*.

Relationship with God in living faith and trust begins
there.

2

Faith and life

Some people find it hard to respond to the truth of
justification by faith, because they have not understood
faith in the terms already set out. They see justification
by faith as a kind of cheap bargain, whereby we
mentally accept what Jesus Christ did for us in dying
upon the cross, and receive in turn forgiveness of sin and
a position of being counted as righteous before God.
They see this as a transaction done in a moment, with
permanent consequences for our standing before God
and unaffected by the way we live from then on. That
seems all too easy. Of course it is, if faith is simply
believing with our minds certain things about what
Jesus did upon the cross. But if faith is responding to
what Jesus did there, because the Holy Spirit has made it
real to us personally as having been done for us at
incredible cost, and if faith is not one step but a life
commitment for a lasting relationship deeper than the
closest relationship this world knows, then while
justification is indeed imparted in a moment, the
believer cannot and will not look back to return to his
old way of life. As Paul put it, 'Shall we go on sinning, so
that grace may increase? By no means! We died to sin;
how can we live in it any longer?' (Romans 6:1.) True
faith carries forward into life.

What, then, are the claims that God makes on those who believe, and what are the purposes He has for them? We need to know these so that we realize what we are letting ourselves in for. 'Marry in haste and repent at leisure' is the word for those who commit themselves unthinkingly to life's deepest tie. How much more when eternal issues hang in the balance! First of all, Abraham learnt that faith means *separation*. He lived in a prosperous city, a place where his father may have had a good business and where material benefits were considerable. He had family links there and friends as well. Response in faith to the Word of God meant being prepared to sever those links and to go out on a dangerous journey to a place he had never seen. He was to be different from other people. He was to have a different life-style and to accept different values—values that from now on would be dictated, not by the views of his contemporaries, but by the demands of a deeper relationship. He was going to have to leave behind all his know-how and be dependent on God for daily provision. And he had no previous experience of this Person who had spoken to him, to know whether he could really rely upon Him.

The extent of the difficulty in taking the first step of separation is found in the fact that from Genesis 11:31 it looks as though Abraham's father Terah shared his faith and took the family out of Ur and into Haran. They were aiming to go to the land of Canaan, to which eventually God would lead Abraham, but somehow they never reached there. Once in Haran, they felt they had gone far enough and settled there and made no more progress until Terah died. They had begun well, but then they began to wonder if God really wanted total commitment and whether they really could face a lifetime of uncertain material provision. Perhaps God did not mean them to change their life-style that much after all. Perhaps if they had moved out of the worst parts of Ur they could live for God safely in Haran. I do not know if I am right about their thinking. I do know that many Christians respond in enthusiasm to the first joy of God's coming to them and for a time live in the warmth of that joy. But when the cross begins to demand changes in life-style, abandonment of some previous ambitions, and a life ruled by the claims of God rather than the standards of surrounding society, then they settle for less. They have gone so far and wonder if it really is necessary to go any further. Surely God will be content with the place we have already reached. Such people never go any further, only moving on when they die! In the meantime the church loses her cutting edge and looks for all the world like a club for those who happen to be 'religious', whatever that means.

Faith does require separation. The extent of it depends on our previous life and on God's purposes for our present one. Everything sinful and evil has to go for a start. Sometimes other things will need to go, too, and not always bad things. For some of us it will involve literally getting up and leaving home and loved ones to go to some other place. The exact details of what is involved are not important. What does matter is that life from now on is dictated by the requirements of an overriding relationship with the Creator of the universe, rather than our own desires or the views of our contemporaries. Faith is prepared for that. The encouraging part of Abraham's story is that he was seventy-five when he set out from Haran. We may have settled for a very long time, or we may have never begun the life of faith, but it is never too late to start.

Secondly, faith for Abraham meant *finding out the purpose of God for his life.* The Lord said, 'Go to the land I will show you.' Notice that God did not tell him where that land was. He was to begin a journey and rely on God to show him each step of the way and to lead him at last to a final destination. He was content for God to do just that, so much so that we are told in Hebrews 11:10 that even at the end of his life he was still looking forward 'to the city with foundations, whose architect and builder is God'. Faith was not only a once-for-all commitment made in a moment, but also a journey towards the fulfilment of God's purposes in his life. This sense of purpose is something really exciting in a world jaded through lack of challenge and lack of anything for which to live or die. Every believer is called to set out on an unknown journey with God to fulfil a purpose that only He knows and to see that purpose unfold day by day and year by year. We never know what turns there may be in the road, but we do know that the Guide knows the way and is sure of the destination, a destination that lies even beyond the end of our lives. This sense of purpose is one of the immense riches of the life of faith.

We live in a world that has lost all sense of purpose. Instead of looking forward with hope to what lies ahead, modern man sees himself caught up in a machine that was set going millions of years ago and in which he is just a cog. The machine is going nowhere, and soon the individual will be worn out and replaced by another cog. He dare not look ahead, for there the prospects are awesome in the extreme, so, 'Let's eat, drink and be merry, for tomorrow we die.' In that context, God comes with His Word of purpose and plan and sovereign control, lifting us out of the machine idea into a world where a personal relationship does count, and where He will lead us to the fulfilment He has already designed.

Thirdly, faith for Abraham meant that *God was going to make something out of him.* 'I will make you into a great nation,' He said (Genesis 12:2). God the Creator is always about His work and nothing delights Him more than taking the rough stuff of human clay and making something beautiful from it. Part of His commitment to us in the life of faith is to do just that. Moreover, God does not mass produce people. He hand carves them. God did not simply mean transmigration for Abraham, but transformation in the process. God's purpose in this world is the creation of a new humanity, and each person in that new humanity is a new creature. So, inevitably, the response of faith to the call of God means placing ourselves in His hands for Him to make us what He wants us to be. Such a purpose for Abraham involved other people, too, for he was to become a great nation. Abraham was not to be a 'self-made' man, for God was going to do the making, just as the Prodigal Son in the parable had to learn to say, 'Make me . . .' before he could be restored to his place in the home. The process of making, like the process of leading, was a lifelong activity. Even when Abraham died, the 'nation' was a tiny community, but God had begun something that was to continue through history. Paul, in writing to the Philippians, expressed his confidence that 'he who began a good work in you will carry it on to completion until the day of Christ Jesus'. God is still taking individuals and making them what He wants them to be as a part of the great new humanity that He is creating. We must therefore be prepared to be made, and that may sometimes be a painful process. It is, however, integral to the life of faith.

The fourth aspect of the life of faith for Abraham was that *God promised to bless him*. The new relationship was a relationship of love and, surrounded by that love, Abraham need have no fears about his welfare. Someone was taking care of it all the time. God would add many things into Abraham's life. God would prosper him in different ways, and by no means always in material terms. God's constant attitude to Abraham would be a positive one. Paul expresses the idea perfectly in Romans 8:32 as far as Christian believers are concerned. 'He who did not spare his own Son, but gave him up for us all—how will he not also, along with him, graciously give us all things?' When God has given the best He has to give, we need have no fear that He will hold back on the rest. The whole idea of blessing someone has an ancient ring to modern ears, but translated into everyday terms it means that God cannot stop giving and He cannot stop loving. Therefore, however dark our circumstances, we can come back to the solid fact that God gave His all at Calvary, so he is not about to leave us in the lurch now.

Part of this blessing that Abraham was to receive was that God would make his name great. God would personally look after Abraham's reputation. Today we still honour Abraham's name, thousands of years after his death. God has made his name great. During his lifetime he had a reputation for riches and was probably known as a man of some standing, but his real greatness has only emerged over the years, until we can now see the full significance of his character and his relationship with God. The greatness God gives is no passing glory. Men make names for themselves and call others great, but God passes the final verdict. Very often the true value of a life is not seen until many years later, when someone whom his contemporaries ignored or rejected is found to be the person who was the greatest. A woman came to Jesus with love in her heart and broke a box of precious ointment and poured it out upon Him. He said that her story would be told all over the world, and it is still being told today. When we leave our reputation in the hands of God we do not have to worry about it.

God then promised Abraham a fifth result of his new-found faith relationship and that was that *he would be a blessing* (Genesis 12:2). The full cup was to overflow to others. No true blessing of God ever comes for purely selfish enjoyment. That is why those who run from convention to convention or from meeting to meeting, seeking the ultimate experience that will lift them above all struggle, are doomed to disappointment. The divine law is 'Give and it shall be given you.' Share what you already have, and God will give you more. In John 7:37-39 Jesus invited the thirsty to come and drink, but He never said in so many words in that passage that those who did so would be satisfied themselves. What He did say was that they would become a source of blessing to others because of the inner spring that the Holy Spirit provides. God does not bless people so that they can say how well off they are. He wants His blessings shared, for it is His nature to share all the good things of the universe.

Once again, the nature of the blessing is personal: 'You will be a blessing.' God wants to multiply people who, because of what they are and what they have received from Him, can reach out to other people in their need. In the West today we live in rapidly disintegrating societies. People have plenty of goods, but little of the good life. Men and women are on edge with each other. Relationships in industry and home grind

away. Many are lonely. Many more are haunted by
deep insecurity. In this context, God looks for those who
can be channels of healing and who in themselves can be
a blessing to others. There is nothing self-conscious in
this. The high-powered 'do-gooder', who provokes such
a hostile reaction today, is not in view here. Rather, the
perfectly natural result of God's blessing in a life is that
that person begins to bring healing and help to others.
He does not have to screw himself up into a good mood
to force himself to do something. The blessing that flows
from a truly Christian life is simply the overflowing work
of the Holy Spirit who lives in that person. Not that he
will sit down and do nothing until he feels some inner
urge, but that the true presence of the Holy Spirit
inevitably results in natural rather than unnatural
blessing to others. The really sad thing in the churches
today is that we often go in and out with minimal
contact with each other and thereby cut off any
possibility of God using us to help each other.

Abraham soon learnt, as we all do, that the life of faith
does not guarantee freedom from problems. Some of
life's pitfalls we do avoid because of the standards that
come into our lives, but as against these there are new
problems with which other people do not have to cope.
Abraham went out with his family and spent the rest of
his life wandering through a strange land among a semi-
hostile people who found him hard to understand. Some
people liked him and responded positively with
blessings, but others had no time for him and replied
with curses. People find Christians hard to understand
at times. Some appreciate the stand we take and
respond warmly, but others hate everything we stand
for and spare no words in telling us so. God told
Abraham how to react in such situations and made it

clear that *the life of faith brings us under God's protection*. He
said, 'I will bless those who bless you, and whoever
curses you I will curse' (Genesis 12:3). God did not
promise freedom from curses. What He did say was that
the person cursing the believer does himself more harm
than he does the believer, because God will turn his
curse round on his own head. God has His own ways of
protecting His people against the hostility of those who
hate them, but the person who does the attacking
exposes himself to the disintegrating effect of his own
hatred. We know something today of the terrible effects
of hatred on the psychological balance and even
physical health of the human frame. Jesus, as He was
nailed to the cross prayed, 'Father, forgive them, for
they do not know what they are doing.' He was
expressing His concern for the real harm His tormentors
were calling upon themselves and their families. Sheer
self-interest should make people hesitate before
attacking God's people.

There remains one more fruit of the life of faith to be
considered. Abraham discovered that response to God's
call to walk with Him involved *infinite expansion in his life*.
God said, 'All peoples on earth will be blessed through
you' (Genesis 12:3). This must have seemed a bit far-
fetched to him at the time. Surely God was doing just a
little bit of exaggerating. We know, however, that God,
as always, was speaking the absolute truth and this book
is being written because God has fulfilled His promise to
Abraham in my life, though I live thousands of years
later in a place of which Abraham had never heard. The
tide of blessing still flows around the world.
Unfortunately, we often shrink from response to the call
of God to a life of faith or a step of obedience, because we
are afraid that our lives will become narrowed down,

impoverished and limited. That is the devil's lie. God's plan for His people is infinite expansion and extension, so that our own lives can become a blessing far beyond our own place where we live and reaching to the ends of the world. God's vision is not limited to certain places. He loves the world and He intends every believer to share that love as widely. Right here, so early in the record of God's revelation to man, we find the seeds of the missionary movement. Every Christian is meant to be a world Christian. Too often, overseas mission is reckoned as an optional extra for those who 'think like that', and in a day when the needs of our own countries are so great we can take the limited view that 'Charity begins at home.' That may be where it begins, but if we are to fulfil our calling in the life of faith, then we have to enlarge our vision to include the world. By placing a limit to our interests, we narrow down our own lives. We cannot, of course, all be involved in travel to other parts of the world, but we can all become involved in prayer and support for those who do go and for the churches that already exist in so many places. In our personal lives, too, God plans for growth and expansion. Abraham grew with his faith. The wizened, crabby creature that picks at this and that and spreads gloom and bitterness around him is a travesty of the Christian life. Faith in an infinite God means infinite expansion for those who belong to Him.

We saw early on in this chapter that faith begins with God and His Word and, as we have looked at the word that God addressed to Abraham as He called him out from Ur, we have seen that it contained in outline many of the ingredients that go to make up a life of faith. We can now go on to see how Abraham's walk with God developed into an ever-deepening friendship. I hope we have seen already that faith is no magical gift that some people happen to have, much as some people can play the piano. It is rooted in a message that we can all find in the pages of the Bible, but it is also based on a real confrontation between ourselves and the living God. This starts a new relationship with Him and opens up all the exciting possibilities for growth and enrichment of personality contained in the promises to make us, bless us, make us a blessing, protect us and expand us, if we will pay the price of committing ourselves wholly to Him and of being ready to be different from the mass of our contemporaries. For most of them, confined in a mechanistic and materialistic prison, God is a massive irrelevancy. Abraham knew, and I trust we also know, the truth to be different. We must show it in our lives.

3

Faith and the two worlds

A new Christian does not have to live very long before he or she realizes with a crunch that the gospel does not solve all our problems overnight. Rather, we begin to cope with a different set of problems and in a new way. One of the biggest disappointments may well arise within the community of God's people, the church. Why do so many people seem to have so little spiritual life? How can people just go through the motions, Sunday by Sunday, and not share in the thrill of a new relationship with God in Christ? Why do so many people seem to be a drag on the church instead of an impetus? Right away this new Christian is facing the problem of the two worlds in which life has to be lived. One is the world in which all men live and for which the church appears to be just another kind of organization to which people may or may not belong. The other is the world of spiritual reality in which God is real and alive and for which the church is the people of God, a community created by Him for His glory and to give to Him the worship that is His due. You have to be spiritually reborn to experience and to enjoy this second world, and indeed Jesus told Nicodemus you cannot 'see' it, that is, be aware of its existence without rebirth by the Spirit of God. The Christian has to live in both of these worlds and they overlap. So some people belong to the church as an organization without belonging to the spiritual community of God, and Christians continue to live in the ordinary everyday world while at the same time being aware of the spiritual one.

Abraham was fully aware of the spiritual world. He had heard the call of God and responded to it. Genesis 12:4 says, 'So Abram left, as the Lord had told him.' Lot, however, was different. He just went with Abraham. He was one of those who linked up with the community of God without really belonging to it in his heart. Between Abraham's journey in obedience and Lot's journey tagging along with the rest there lies a huge gulf. The one went in response to a call from God, with a purpose reinforced by conviction. The other went because it was the socially accepted thing to do. The people of God have always been plagued by such hangers-on, and they always will be because the two worlds exist side by side. There are still those who go along with the people of God but whose faith never seems to make too much difference to their attitudes and actions. They are not conscious of going anywhere in particular. They are not aware of walking with God through life and are not too interested in what heaven is all about at the end. Like Lot they just go along. We shall hear more of the problems that Lot caused. On the other hand, let us remember that the Lord Jesus told us in the parable of the tares and wheat that His kingdom would always contain a mixed community and human attempts at the present time to sort out the true from the false usually end in disaster. If only people had heeded this warning we might have been spared the numerous attempts to form the perfect church that have often led to bitterness and division.

A second problem that a new Christian soon faces is the relationship of his or her new-found faith to relatives and especially to children. This question becomes particularly acute when obedience to the will of God involves the financial security, life-style or welfare of children too young to know what is happening and unable to take part in the decision. Here we can take courage from the fact that Sarah and numerous other relatives were involved in Abraham's response to God's call. Whether we like it or not, a person's response and obedience inevitably involve those who are nearest and dearest. This is true whether those relatives have entered into a personal response and obedience themselves or not. God deals with families as well as with individuals. The Bible is an Eastern book. Families count as units in the East. Atomized individualism is Greek and Western, not biblical and Eastern. So those of us in the West have a particular problem here.

We have had to face this problem in our own family, for God called us to serve Him overseas in Asia. The call involved us and our children in many new experiences and in separations that normally would not have come to us. As they have grown older, the children have come to accept for themselves their part in God's call, but we could no more have asked them about it in the first place than Abraham could have asked 'the people they had acquired in Haran' whether they would like to go, too. We had to make a decision when only one of our children was alive, and Abraham had to decide many years before Isaac came along what he would do. We do not find the separation from our children easy, and nor do they. What makes it harder still, however, is the accusation that sometimes comes to us that Scripture never countenances such separation, and that it is almost immoral to make a decision affecting the family unless they are all of age and freely give their consent. God is fully aware of family circumstances when He makes His will known to individuals and we have to trust His wisdom in this as in everything else. No person is an island. Our lives are bound together with those around us. We cannot act totally in isolation. Therefore when we come to trust in the Lord, those around us are going to be affected in one way or another and we have to accept that. Certainly complications cannot be avoided, especially if a wife or husband has not yet come to the same experience that is so real to us.

A third area in which we are made acutely conscious of the two worlds in which we live is in relating to the world outside, whether that be in school, office, factory or shop. Lilly is a person who illustrates this perfectly. A temporary resident in England, where she was working as a nurse in an intensive care unit, one day she saw a copy of *Good News for Modern Man* on a friend's table. She had not really taken much notice of the Bible before, but she picked up this book and began to read. Then she found she could not put it down. When the time came to return to her lodgings, the friend told her to take the book with her. She read it all the way home on the bus and on into the early hours of the morning. Then at around 2.30 a.m. she slipped out of bed and gave her life to the Lord who had so clearly spoken to her from His Word. Full of her new-found faith and joyfully wanting to share what had happened, she innocently told her friends at work, only to be shaken to the core by their response. 'Lilly has got religion.' 'You will soon get over that, Lilly. We all go through that at some time or another.' No one seemed to be able to share the reality of her experience. Then they began to urge her and press

her to swear and blaspheme in the common
conversation of the day. The more they pressed, the
more she found she could not bring herself to do it, and
the unhappier she became that no one seemed to be able
to understand. The experience of God through His Word
in the middle of the night was crystal clear to her. Yet so
was the pressure of her ordinary everyday environment.

Abraham faced the same problem. Abraham moved
out of Ur and came into the land of Canaan. He had
been obedient to the command to leave his home and
move out. So he arrived in the new land, the land that he
had been promised for himself, only to find that 'the
Canaanites were then in the land' (Genesis 12:6.) Of
course, he had known with his head before he left home
that people of a different culture and outlook would be
living 'over there', but knowing it in theory and rubbing
shoulders with them in practice were two very different
things. The Canaanites did not accept the reality of
Abraham's God. They practised a form of nature
worship, allied to the need for fertility in their fields.
Such worship often involved ritual prostitution and
worship at local idol shrines. The Canaanites did not
accept Abraham's call, and they certainly did not
believe that the God he worshipped had any right to
give their land to this newcomer. Who did he think he
was, anyway? He lived like them in some ways, and yet
in others he was different. Was he trying to show them
up and set himself up as some judge of other people's
morals? Why did he have to behave differently? Such
behaviour made them feel uncomfortable when they
had felt at ease before. He was a foreigner and
interloper. He was the one who was different. Why
could he not be reasonable and behave like one of
themselves? Why should they listen to him?

At times Abraham must have wondered about his original call. God had not told him it would be quite like this. Every Christian knows exactly how he felt. The new dimension of reality we know as Christians, the spiritual world, is as real and relevant to our contemporaries as 'ghosties and ghoulies and things that go bump in the night'. They do not understand us. Our God is to them an unreal phantasy of our imagination, our standards are foreign and our differences puzzling or even offensive. Who are these people who do not fit? The world seems to be able to accommodate all kinds of nonconformists and a wide variety of religions. But the one exception is the believer in the true God. He attracts and often receives a hostility out of all proportion to his ideas. Let us not be surprised, therefore, when the warm experience of coming to know God in Christ and sharing that experience with other Christians is paralleled by puzzlement and even persecution from friends to whom the Christian way of life is foreign.

Just at this point we read, 'The Lord appeared to Abram and said, "To your offspring I will give this land."' The Canaanites represented practical down-to-earth reality. The Word of God represented spiritual and none the less potent reality. For the Christian, one is as real as the other and we have to live with both. The first cold douche of frozen unfriendliness from his new environment was met for Abraham by a fresh sense of the Lord's presence, not this time back in the comfort and safety of Ur, but right there in the harsh reality of Canaanite rejection. God is very gracious. He comes to us at our point of need and underlines His presence with fresh assurances, and we need them. God has to come to us and say, 'Yes, despite all appearances, I have put you here and I intend to accomplish My purposes, be the unbelieving crowd around you never so unresponsive or rejecting.' Practical reality has to be balanced by spiritual reality.

Abraham's response at this point was to build 'an altar to the Lord, who had appeared to him', right there in Canaan. Renewed commitment expressed in worship and dedication sealed Abraham's determination to go on. He could so easily have crumpled and compromised. Many Christians do just that. The practical reality overwhelms the spiritual and remains the dominant force. This should not be. For the Christian both realities should be alive. We cannot ignore the practical reality without leaving our head in the clouds. We cannot forget the spiritual reality without fastening irons to our feet. God told Abraham at this point that the *status quo* is not unalterable. One day Abraham's descendants would own that very land and be able to change it into what it was meant to be. The attainment of the ideal might be far in the future, and only Abraham's descendants might see it, but come it would and God works to an eternal time-scale. Abraham might not see any way to reach the ideal and the Canaanites were very real. But that did not matter. The power of the Lord was stronger than the power of the Canaanites. The power of the Lord is still stronger than the anti-Christian forces that surround us today. And the patience of the Lord is greater than the impatience of any of His servants. Our job, as Abraham's was, is to respond to the Lord in the middle of hostile environments with a renewed response and dedication that commit us to go on with Him. The old sense of call is not enough. We need the assurance that 'this land', whatever and wherever it may be, with all its resident 'Canaanites' is a place to be claimed for the kingdom of God.

Abraham did not screw himself up to make this renewed response by a cold act of the will. God was real to him there in that land. He erected the altar in response to an appearance. Formal, ritual altars, that bear no relation to living experiences of God, are heaps of dry stones. Abraham's worship was living and wherever he went he worshipped, creating in each place concrete evidence of his faith in God (Genesis 12:7-9). This kind of faith that lives day by day in relationship with God is God's plan for every Christian. Each morning we can erect in our homes and hearts a new altar of worship and obedience that keeps alive our sense of spiritual reality and enables us to face the challenges of the new day. We need this daily reminder of God's presence with us. I find in our modern world that some Christians, in reaction against dead formalism, have abandoned the practice of a morning 'quiet time'. I can understand their fear of formalism. I cannot understand their abandonment of the worship of God. When we live among the Canaanites we need the assurance of the appearance of God.

Our generation is impatient of tradition and ritual and therefore needs convincing that the regular Sunday worship of the church of God has any meaning. Yet it is in the context of the two worlds in which Christians live that we need not only the personal and individual worship of God and reading of His Word, but also the corporate worship where we can spend more time and where we can listen to His Word expounded and explained to us. Worshipping with others warms our hearts with the reminder that, however lonely we may be in our Christian outlook from Monday to Saturday, we are not alone in experiencing the reality of the grace of God, but part of a world-wide community spread, not only across the globe, but right down the pages of history, too. If we belong to a group that makes use of the Creed, we can remind ourselves when we say, 'I believe . . .' that millions have lived and died in this conviction and still do.

As Abraham moved around the land, he erected one altar after another, as though he were saying that in each place he was claiming that place for God. God had said the land would be his, and Abraham expressed his conviction that this promise was not just words by worshipping the Lord wherever he went. And he travelled all over the land, even to the southernmost limits of the Negev. Never did he settle down. He 'set out and continued towards . . .'. It was as though calling upon the name of the Lord in a place made it peculiarly God's and therefore Abraham's, too. There is an important spiritual truth here. Whether we be a missionary claiming some hitherto unbelieving people for God, or a Christian claiming territory in his own personality for Him, we can never stop moving on. There is always more progress to be made. That progress is made from day to day. Walk and worship, walk and worship, are evidence of a life of faith.

Abraham began with the call of God to come and walk with Him through life. Sensing a new dimension, Abraham responded to the call and very soon found that he lived in two worlds, worlds that were often in conflict with each other. They were present in his family and among the people to whom he went, and they brought to him new problems he had not had to cope with before. But Abraham persevered because of the intense reality of the God who had called him and because he maintained a relationship with that same God in regular communion and worship. We cannot expect to avoid the problems that living in two worlds brings to us as Christians. Yet we have the Holy Spirit and the full revelation of the Word of God to enable us to persevere through living fellowship with the Lord Himself. The question is, how far we are prepared to put ourselves out to maintain the regular pattern of walk and worship day by day.

4

Faith and famine

To hear some evangelists preach, you would think that
the Christian life was easy. 'Come to Christ,' they say,
'and all your problems will be solved. He will give you
peace of heart, forgiveness of sins, meaning in life,
guidance to glory, and everything you need on the way.'
There is enough truth in this offer to make it dangerous.
The problem lies not so much in what is said, as in what
is left out. Jesus in His call to discipleship talked rather of
a cross and a cost, without which to follow Him is
pointless. He learned obedience by the things that He
suffered and He knew what He was talking about. The
trouble with the modern offer is that when the going gets
tough we feel hurt, deceived and even despairing. This is
not what we were promised.

We left Abraham pressing on in faith to the
southernmost part of the country. Walking with God
day by day, he worshipped and rejoiced. Then verse 10
of chapter 12 produces a sudden jarring note of discord:
'Now there was a famine in the land.' In the selfsame
land to which God had directed Abraham, there was a
famine. What was He doing? Not only was there a
famine, but a severe one at that. So the Lord had taken a
man and called him to sacrifice the comfort and ease of
Ur, to go to a special promised land, and when He had

got him there, He seemingly left him to starve. Abraham now had the promise of becoming a great nation, but no son, and the promise of a land, but no sustenance. All he had was a barren wife and a barren wilderness. I am sure that if we have been Christians more than a very short time we know how Abraham felt. What on earth was God doing?

The lesson is plain. The place of God's appointment does not exclude shortage, affliction or problems. Job was God's man. Hosea loved his Lord. Jeremiah was a faithful servant. They all suffered. Shall we be the exceptions? The Christian life is not a fortress but a furnace, not a vacation but a vocation, not a rest but a wrestling with spiritual forces of evil. The fulness of God's blessing does not exclude the scarcity of God's famine. Men like George Müller and Hudson Taylor could testify in financial matters that, for all God's wonderful and constant provision, there were times when they did not know where their next meal would come from. And many of the Lord's most special servants through history can testify to 'the dark night of the soul' through which they have passed on more than one occasion. 'Famine in the land' does not contradict God's real promises, but only the myths of men, who have imagined that he who is in the will of God cannot possibly find himself at the end of his resources.

Abraham's reaction was similar to what ours usually is. He decided to move, to look for his own food, to find temporary relief in doing something. Like Peter walking on the water, he began to look around instead of looking up. By staying on, he stood to lose. By trusting God in the middle of a famine, he might become totally bankrupt. Here was a test whether he really did believe that God intended the very best for him. Was God's

Word trustworthy without outward confirmation, or was he relying on the confirmation, not the Word?

Abraham's action was perfectly rational. He could not support his family without provisions. By moving he could obtain the provision that God seemed to be withholding. It was the obvious thing to do. As obvious as turning the stones into bread must have appeared to Jesus in the wilderness. But more than bread was at stake. Can man really rely on the living God to meet his every need? Can he depend on the Lord's ability and on His love? Jesus answered, 'Yes, he can.' Abraham voted with his feet; fled for refuge to Egypt and failed the test.

How else can God deepen our trust in His unseen presence and love, except by placing us in situations which demand trust solely in Him and in *nothing else*? That is how we learn that He is really there. That is why Jesus flatly refused the devil's suggestion that, as the Son of God, He should behave independently of God and turn stones into bread on His own account. He answered, 'Man does not live on bread alone, but on every word that comes from the mouth of God' (Matthew 4:4). The real nature of man is that of a dependent creature who must rely upon his Creator and trust Him absolutely if he is to live in the way he was meant to do. Adam and Eve had been warned not to take their destiny into their own hands and eat the forbidden fruit, but the devil had promised them that if they did they could be 'like God, knowing good and evil' (Genesis 3:5). He was promising them independence of the Creator and ever since that time man has had an inbuilt bias to self-centred independence. Jesus in the temptation was reversing the trend and therefore refused to use His God-given powers to solve His own food problem without reference to God's way of doing it.

When Abraham went down into Egypt he was following the way of Adam. We can hardly blame him, for we do the same so often ourselves. What we can learn from this incident is that when God brings us into a situation where we see no solution and where we are tempted to opt out, we must ask ourselves, 'Has God brought me here to learn to trust Him implicitly when there is nothing else to trust and nothing else left?'

Maybe someone reading this is thinking of pulling out. Perhaps it is from some missionary situation; perhaps from some strained relationship. Maybe you even feel slightly bitter that God has by His call and guidance landed you in this mess. The possibility of no fruit and no provision never entered your head when He called. Now everything else is gone. Only the Lord is left. Here is the crunch. Do you really believe and trust Him, or only say you do? God is trusting you with a chance to prove Him. The temptation came to Jesus just after a marvellous experience of the coming of the Holy Spirit upon Him at His baptism. The famine came to Abraham just after starting out on his walk with God and when he had left behind all the ties that bound him to his old way of life. He had gone too far to go back and in a sense was out on a limb. Many a Christian has faced an identical experience. Some of us have come out from difficult circumstances such as drugs or alcoholism or a broken home, and the first experience of Jesus Christ and the power of His Spirit was just wonderful. But then things have settled down, and added to the testing of seeming barrenness has come the backlash of old problems, the effects of which still dog our feelings. We are tempted to doubt the reality of the first experience and we are tested whether we are really trusting God or our experiences. The enemy tempts us to destroy us, but

God is testing us to strengthen us, so that we might prove Him to be really there, even in the darkness. We are not alone in facing such times and we need to share our feelings with our brothers and sisters in Christ so that we can discover that we are neither unique in our perplexity, nor peculiar in our doubts.

Every missionary knows the stripped feeling of the first two years in a new country and a new culture. All the ministry, meetings, fellowship and usefulness that kept us going before we came out have been taken away. We are left alone, as babes in a new world, and often like babes in the wood. We feel useless and helpless and think back to all that we used to be able to do, but now we can do nothing. And then it is that we realize the truth of that old saying: 'What a man or woman is on their knees before God, that they are and no more.' The shattering part is that what we are is found to be precious little. There is a famine in the land and we want out. Certainly none of us has any stones handy to throw at Abraham.

At times like these we are tempted to fall back into rationalism. As Christians, we are not meant to behave irrationally, but rationalism is that way of thinking that behaves as though God does not exist, however much we say we believe He does. The modern world is dominated by rationalism. So Abraham reasoned it all out logically. Famine meant loss of cattle and possible loss of life. Egypt was a place where they stored grain for times like these and perhaps the famine was not so bad down there. True, he had been told to go to Canaan and that was the land God had promised him, but God did not seem to be around very much at the moment, and the rational thing to do in solving his own problem was to go down into Egypt as quickly as possible. Having begun to rationalize, Abraham went further. He looked at his

wife and realized a fact—she was beautiful (Genesis
12:11). Like a wise husband, he told her so. But then he
spoilt it. Having begun to doubt God's word and ability,
he could not trust Him in Egypt any more than in
Canaan. As unbelief is usually pessimistic, he made an
unjustified assumption that fitted his mood: 'They will
say, "This is his wife." Then they will kill me but will let
you live.' The assumption of what they would say led
inevitably to the conclusion of what they would do.
Abraham was sure he would not survive. Unbelief has
friends, and one of those friends is fear. Another is self-
pity. Both came to visit Abraham. He could not have
painted a darker picture from his own point of view, and
it seems that it was not too much consolation to him that
Sarah would be allowed to live. So Abraham was cast on
his own cleverness and that somehow came up with
answers much quicker than God did. 'Say you are my
sister,' (well, she was in fact his half-sister) 'so that I will
be treated well for your sake and my life will be spared
because of you.' A half-lie must be a half-truth, so surely
that would not matter!

When Abraham arrived in Egypt, his predictions
were fulfilled and the Egyptians were quick to recognize
his wife's beauty. Now things began to get complicated.
Since Abraham had told them she was his sister, there
was nothing to stop them drawing Pharaoh's attention
to the new arrival and eventually incorporating her into
the number of his wives or potential consorts. Even more
embarrassing were the presents that Abraham received
from the king for bringing this beautiful woman into the
country. 'He treated Abraham well for her sake, and
Abraham acquired sheep and cattle, male and female
donkeys, menservants and maidservants and camels'
(Genesis 12:16). Human reasoning is incapable of

foreseeing all the consequences of our actions, and certainly Abraham had not reckoned on all this. Thinking so much about the danger to his own life, he had hardly spared a thought for what might happen to Sarah if someone took a fancy to her, least of all if that person were none other than the king. The tangled web he had woven when first he began to deceive held him firmly in its grip. He had decided he could not depend upon God's provision in the famine or God's protection in Egypt. He had acted from fear instead of from principle, and he raised a problem that need never have existed. Once we depart from the way of trust and obedience, we find ourselves in trouble. To trust Him sometimes looks the hardest thing to do in the circumstances. In the end trust leads to the least complications. The lie Abraham had told compounded his problems and postponed the crisis that eventually had to come. Problems grow no easier by postponement. They have a high inflation rate.

Fortunately, God does not forsake His people even when they get themselves up to the neck in problems because, instead of trusting Him, they have followed their own way. God intervened directly in the situation and Pharaoh became so uncomfortable that he began to trace the origin of his troubles and found that they all stemmed from the day when he had taken Sarah into the palace. He soon discovered his mistake and rightly felt thoroughly annoyed with Abraham: '"What have you done to me?" he said. "Why didn't you tell me she was your wife? Why did you say, 'She is my sister', so that I took her to be my wife? Now then, here is your wife. Take her and go!"' (Genesis 12:18.) Then we are told that 'Pharaoh gave orders about Abraham to his men, and they sent him on his way, with his wife and everything he had.' Thrown out on his ear from the place that he had thought would be a secure refuge from the famine, Abraham slunk away in shame to face the same problem from which he had first run away. He certainly survived, so he could have done so if he had stayed, but through lack of trust in the God who had called him he wandered into a quagmire of difficulty.

Abraham faced two problems in this incident. One we have already looked at as Abraham failed to trust God in a position of famine. The other problem was the one of personal relationships. Here he had failed, too, by being unwilling to be straightforward and open. Unfortunately Christians are not always as honest in these areas as some who make no profession of faith. Certainly Pharaoh comes out of the incident with considerably more honour than the man of God. Are we sometimes afraid of hurting people if we are honest with them? Are we afraid of what they will think of us if we tell them the truth? We do well to learn that in personal relationships a problem seized is a problem solved and a problem skirted is a problem multiplied.

Abraham first landed himself in trouble by losing sight of God in the midst of his circumstances. Then in the ensuing pessimism he looked at the facts of life, made assumptions and drew the worst conclusions. Then he created devices to get round things and gave himself good reasons for using them. But let us not be too hard on Abraham. He had an agonizing decision to make. He had more than seventy people for whom he was responsible. Real faith is needed to take the hard road when it seems to lead to certain failure. I think of some Asian Christians in the agony of deciding whether to leave their own homeland or not. If they stay they expect Communism to come, or something just as bad.

They have families to bring up and care for, and yet
their countries need the witness of Jesus Christ, too, and
they are nationals who can remain whatever happens. I
think of someone in a well-paid job who knows that the
kind of things he is asked to do are contrary to the truth
of God and yet who knows that if he gives up his job he
may never find another. I think of another who is sure
God means him to give up his present work and spend
all his time in a Christian ministry, but who has a family
and a mortgage and other commitments. Deciding is no
light or easy thing. Walking closely with God can alone
enable right conclusions.

Abraham's self-made solution turned out to be no
solution at all. Somewhere down in Egypt, Sarah took
on a new maid called Hagar. Perhaps she was given to
her during her stay in the palace and left Egypt with her.
Hagar became the mother of Ishmael and Sarah the
mother of Isaac. We still live with the consequences in
the Middle East today. From small seeds come big trees.
We are left saying, 'If only . . .' But then we all have our
stock of 'if onlys' in the cupboard. The important thing
to remember is that God did not abandon Abraham
because he made this mistake, serious as it was. He still
went on to become known as the friend of God. We all
stumble and fall, and have to remind ourselves that our
acceptance does not depend on always doing the right
thing, but solely on the righteousness we receive through
the cross of Christ. We can come back to that cross again
and again for cleansing and then we must get up and go
on.

5

Faith and family quarrels

When we are new believers we are often thrilled with our first experiences of Christian fellowship, especially if we are received into a warm community where most of the people attending have a living relationship with Jesus Christ. On the other hand, there inevitably comes a time when we are forcibly reminded that the church is a congregation of sinners, even if they are saved by grace. The life of faith does not provide automatic or easy answers to problems of personal relationships. A naive impression that Christians should not have problems of personal relationships can make us less able to cope with them because then a readiness to admit failure, or even the existence of a problem, can seem to be a betrayal of our faith in the Lord. At that point we can pretend that everything is all right when everyone around us knows that it is not. We can also pretend to be better than in fact we are, for fear of letting God down.

The fact is that Christians, like all people, have problems of personal relationships both within our own families and within the family of God's people, let alone outside. The question is *how we deal with them and what we allow them to do to us*. When we move into Genesis 13 we find Abraham facing a family difference. He found that he had a quarrel on his hands, and he used that quarrel

as a means of spiritual growth. Conflict in our lives may
be used for growth in maturity or sliding into bitterness.
The difference that his faith made to Abraham in his
quarrel with Lot consisted in the perspective from which
he could view the problem, not in the provision of a
simple magic answer. Abraham was able to look at his
problem in the light of God's loving care for him, in the
context of God's promises to him and in the dimension of
God's time-scale. That was what made the difference.
Instead of reacting emotively to the accusations that
began flying around, Abraham took a good long look at
God's way of viewing things. That is not an easy thing to
do, especially in the early days of a life of faith, because
we have inbuilt responses that have been triggered so
many times in similar circumstances, and in the heat of
the argument we lose our perspective unless we give
ourselves time to think. We need a cooling-off period.
Paul tells us in Romans 12:2 to 'be transformed by the
renewing of your mind'. That takes time and discipline,
but it does enable us to view even our conflicts
differently. Again, this is a compelling reason for daily
study of the Word of God and communion with Him in
prayer, for the heat of the moment in a quarrel simply
spills out what is inside us already and if there is not very
much of God's thinking running around our minds, we
cannot expect to produce right responses.

Before we look at the problem facing Abraham and
Lot, we should note one significant sentence in verse 7 of
chapter 13: 'The Canaanites and Perizzites were also
living in the land at that time.' This comment may be
included to show that Abraham and Lot did not have
the place to themselves and therefore could not use
unlimited pastures, but it may also be there to underline
the fact that other people were watching their

behaviour. Their quarrel will not have gone unnoticed. Certainly, whatever believers do, they do before a watching world—a world only too quick and too happy to point out the inconsistencies of those who claim a relationship with God. In a world torn apart by problems of personal relationships, people watch carefully to see if Jesus Christ makes a difference at that crucial point.

The quarrel between Abraham and Lot did not actually begin with them. We read that 'quarrelling arose between Abraham's herdsmen and the herdsmen of Lot'. The natural tendency in such a case is for the principals to take up the cudgels on behalf of the agents. Of course, we do not have to do this, and some sad differences could be avoided if parents did not automatically take up their children's defence, or leaders of organizations did not necessarily take up their members' grievances. I remember a serious difference between a missionary and the national head of a Bible College that arose because the missionary took up the cause of a student who had been refused admission. He had been a person in whom she had been particularly interested, but really there was no need for disagreement, for the young man was not ready for such studies. We must be careful before we fight on someone else's behalf.

Quarrels do not begin without some cause. There is no smoke without a fire. In dealing with them, therefore, we should first of all *seek to discover the basic cause for the differences that have arisen*. The cause tends to be forgotten when people become heated. In the case of Abraham and Lot, the original starting-point was basically that a change in their respective material circumstances had made the place just too small to take both of them. When they had set out at first, they had few enough

cattle to pasture them alongside each other without
friction. But in Genesis 13:2 we read, 'Abraham had
become very wealthy in livestock and in silver and gold.'
Verses 5 and 6 say, 'Now Lot, who was moving about
with Abram, also had flocks and herds and tents. But the
land could not support them while they stayed together,
for their possessions were so great that they were not able
to stay together.' Material affluence does not solve our
problems, but presents us with a new set. A farm that
supports three hundred head of cattle cannot necessarily
support a thousand. Of course, the change in material
possessions had not happened overnight. That was why
they had not noticed what that change was doing to
their relationship. Gradual changes can alter delicate
balances without our realizing it. So one thing we have
to do is to keep an eye on changes in our lives and
anticipate possible trouble before it reaches explosive
proportions. This is certainly true in the marriage
relationship, but also in many church situations. The
Sunday School that grows from one to four hundred is
going to need some careful handling. The space
available may just not be big enough and teachers are
going to get on each other's nerves. Material
circumstances affect personal relationships, but we may
not notice how they do this unless we are on the alert.

Secondly, we should note that *personal differences are
often made worse by other ingredients in the situation* which
sometimes put more emotional content into it than the
original cause. These are not the cause of the difference,
but irritant factors. Very frequently there is deep
cultural misunderstanding at the root, but the racial
factor adds heat. So in Abraham's case there were two
other elements that may well have made things more
difficult. One of these was the generation gap. Abraham

was probably considerably older than his nephew Lot, and while in those days such a gulf between their ages would not have been as significant as in our day, it was still there. There could have been an element of jealousy there, too, for obviously Abraham was wealthier than Lot. The younger man may have wondered why his uncle should have it all and why his herds should take up more room. In our case, we still need to be alert to the extra irritant factors in any quarrel and to ask ourselves if some of the minor ones are not in fact causing more trouble than the original point at issue.

Another element that certainly affected the final result for the parties concerned was that Lot does not appear to have shared Abraham's call and faith in God in anything like the depth that would have produced deep oneness of outlook. 'Abram left, as the Lord had told him; and Lot went with him.' That is how Genesis 12:4 describes their leaving Haran. Lot had come along for the ride, as it were, and probably did not see why he should go short on pasture. Between the outlooks of these two men lies a great gulf. Abraham was aware of the reality of the unseen, of the firmness of the promises of God, and of His presence with him as he went along. The other man had simply joined in what was going on and was rather impatient with someone who enjoyed a deeper dimension in life and faith to which he himself was a stranger. Such a fundamental difference in outlook and experience of God in church congregations leads to problems that need very careful handling and much spiritual discernment. The person who simply joins in the activities, but whose trust in the Lord does not run deep enough radically to affect life and action, can cause real hindrance to spiritual growth and progress. The church on earth will never be wholly free from such

people who profess the name of Christian, but who are
scarcely distinguishable from the world around.

How then did Abraham respond in this crisis of
relationships? The first thing he did was to *take the
initiative to bring the trouble out into the open and to talk about it*.
He went to Lot and stated his case. Jesus later told us to
do exactly the same. He said, 'If you are offering your
gift at the altar and there remember that your brother
has something against you, leave the gift there in front of
the altar. First go and be reconciled to your brother;
then come and offer your gift' (Matthew 5:23,24). Or
again, 'If your brother sins against you, go and show him
his fault, just between the two of you' (Matthew 18:15).
The trouble is that doing this can be embarrassing. We
would rather save our friend's face and ours, so we
pretend that the problem is not there; but it is, and it will
not go away until we learn that Jesus meant what He
said.

Any fool can start a quarrel. It takes a person of
maturity and stature to take the first step to stop one.
Abraham, as the older and more mature man, had that
responsibility and, to his credit, he discharged it. In
doing so *he acted without heat and on a matter of principle*. He
said to Lot, 'Let's not have any quarrelling between you
and me, or between your herdsmen and mine, *for we are
brothers*.' The principle of kinship took an overriding
place in his thinking and formed a starting-point for
their discussions. A deep-seated relationship existed
between them which gave them every cause for mutual
love rather than quarrelling. Once they started with the
principle, the issues at stake could be seen for the
comparatively trifling ones that they really were. When
we begin with biblical principle we can avoid many
pitfalls.

When Paul was dealing with the party-minded quarrelling church of Corinth, he felt compelled to give some of his deepest teaching on the unity of the Body of Christ. 1 Corinthians 12 is one of the classic passages on this subject, and the hymn of love in chapter 13 emerged from the darkness of a situation where party-minded, petty Christians were even prepared to take each other to court to prove a point. The unity of the Spirit is so frequently the last thought in the mind of Christians who are at odds with each other, when it should be the determining principle. Because Abraham began with the principle, he deduced right at the start that strife had to be out. Christians are as different from each other as any group of men and women. But, whether we like it or not, we *are* brethren, children of the same heavenly Father, born of the same Spirit, saved by the same Lord, and one day we shall be compelled before the judgement seat of Christ to acknowledge the fact, if we will not do it now. Jesus prayed in His great high-priestly prayer of John 17, 'May they be brought to complete unity to let the world know that you sent me and have loved them even as you have loved me' (John 17:23). Because such unity is so strong a witness in a world divided in every direction, it is inevitably the target of attack. We should, therefore, be specially alert that the devices of Satan may not succeed, instead of playing into his hands. Paul exhorted the Ephesians to the same earnest effort to safeguard unity when he wrote to them, 'I urge you to live a life worthy of the calling you have received . . . . Make every effort to keep the unity of the Spirit through the bond of peace. There is one body and one Spirit . . .' (Ephesians 4:1-4).

Preservation of unity involves hard work. No comfortable emotional feeling or experience of spiritual

elation is found in doing it. Rather, it calls for an
attitude which Paul in the same Ephesian passage
describes in these terms: 'Be completely humble and
gentle; be patient, bearing with one another in love'
(Ephesians 4:2). That requires cold, hard, down-to-
earth obedience at times. Judging by the strife-ridden
churches that abound across the world, we have
forgotten the call to unity and the faith we profess in
sharing a common calling. The cross is allowed to
decorate our churches, but not to cut into our
behaviour. Abraham, when he acted on the principle
that he and Lot were kinsmen, had no guarantee that his
nephew would respond in the same way. He was putting
himself at risk by doing that which is right, and leaving
the results with God. What a difference we would see if
enough people did the same!

On the other hand, Abraham did not just have his
head in the clouds. He *recognized reality*. The land just
could not support all the herds and flocks of both men.
They might as well recognize that fact and separate
from each other. A recognition of reality does not mean
admission of defeat. Believers are not meant to be naive.
For two friends to stop sharing a flat, when clearly they
are so different from each other that life becomes
intolerable, may not be accepting failure but
recognizing the truth and acting with plain common
sense. Life brings enough complications without making
martyrs of ourselves when a simple separation can solve
the problem without a lasting breach of relationships. I
am not referring to marriage here, of course. In that case
vows made before God are involved and the time to do
the thinking is before making the commitment. Two
people who have agreed to share a flat are on a totally
different basis.

Having taken the initiative and acted on principle, Abraham having seen the realities of the situation *made a generous gesture*: 'Is not the whole land before you? Let's part company. If you go to the left, I'll go to the right; if you go to the right, I'll go to the left' (Genesis 13:9). He gave Lot the choice. One way was immeasurably more attractive than the other, with richly watered plains on the one hand, and the sparser pasture of the hills on the other. As the older man, Abraham had the right to choose and, as the richer man, he had the more to lose. Nevertheless, he was still willing to give Lot first choice. Here we see something of the growth of this man. Few of us are able to be generous in a controversy and fear of loss triggers defensive mechanisms that destroy openheartedness. But Abraham was not afraid of what he might lose. His inheritance came from God and remained safe in the hands of God. As F. B. Meyer expressed it, Abraham had 'no fear that Lot could ever rob him of that which was guaranteed to him by the faithfulness of God'. He did not walk by faith just on Sundays, and his faith was what set him free to be generous. God was so real to him that he could take his hands off and leave the result to Him. We can become so afraid of losing our little positions, influence, power or status. When they are threatened, we take up the cudgels and find arguments we never realized existed to preserve our hold on everything in sight. It is written of Jesus that He 'did not consider equality with God something to be grasped, but made himself nothing, taking the very nature of a servant' (Philippians 2:6,7). Again, Peter wrote of Him, 'When they hurled their insults at him, he did not retaliate; when he suffered, he made no threats. Instead, he entrusted himself to him who judges justly . . .' (1 Peter

2:23). Jesus had everything to lose when He laid down His life at the cross and for a time He lost it all, but His confidence in His Father was such that He could rely on Him as the Ruler of the universe to do the right thing and not to allow His Son to lose anything in the end. That is what the life of faith is all about. Can we not then let go of our senseless stranglehold on our petty possessions and positions and leave Him to determine our inheritance, even if we do have to lose it all first? Once again we have a reversal of Adam's way of wanting to determine his own destiny and a willingness to rest on the goodness and ability of God who made the world. In a little booklet long out of print, the Rev. Alan Stibbs expressed it in this way for Abraham: 'Lot walked in the limits of his own choosing; Abraham in the length and breadth of God's giving.'

Abraham did not lose anything. God's people never do. When we even think of the possibility of a child of the Creator, even an adopted one, really being in a losing position, it is patently ridiculous. What we may lose is what our contemporaries in the world would consider of value because of their blinkered vision that confines itself to that which can be touched, tasted and handled, and their limited perspective that has no future beyond death. Even if the loss involved includes life itself, we know as Jesus knew that the resurrection provides a complete answer and a full vindication. When it came to the final apportioning, God gave it all to Abraham. In fact, as soon as Lot had disappeared on his way, God said to Abraham, 'Lift up your eyes from where you are and look north and south, east and west. All the land that you see I will give to you and your offspring for ever' (Genesis 13:14,15). The four points of the compass seem to include everywhere, to my way of thinking, so

Abraham was promised possession of even those parts which Lot appeared to have taken for himself. Truly the meek will inherit the earth.

When our concept of God is that of someone whom man has thought up to explain the riddle of the universe, we cannot afford to be generous. He is then little more than a figment of the imagination. Some people may like the idea of such a being and some may not, but we can take our choice. Whichever choice we do make, there is not much difference, for to the man of the world there is nothing 'out there' to correspond with the idea. But the Christian knows differently. The God who is there has come to us, sometimes when we did not want to believe in Him, and now God is the great Reality, the real lover of His universe and of His people. So we can trust this Person with our life, our goods, our family and our future without fear, knowing that in His hands all is safe. We do not necessarily find it easy to do, and we find it especially hard to take our hands off our children, particularly in their teenage years when to us they may seem to be making wrong decisions and when we are the last people whose advice they really appreciate because they are fighting a necessary battle to establish their own identity distinct from ours. Then we are really tested in our trust in God's ability to preserve what we have committed to Him.

Abraham came out of his quarrel with Lot *a much bigger person*. In a short space of time he grew in maturity and spiritual stature to the place where God could safely reveal big plans for the way ahead. Most of us do not reach that stage very quickly because we have not learnt that the important point about a quarrel is not whether we win it, but what it does to our spirit. Abraham was sufficiently rooted in his trust in God to walk with Him

through the pressures. God reveals His secrets to such
people.

By contrast we may look at Lot as he went down to the
plain and lived with the consequences of his own choice.
The quarrel for him led to a long slippery slope that
finally left him the father of a child by each of his
daughters, with his wife dead in tragic circumstances
and with his goods gone. He did not get there in one
downward leap and never intended to get there at all.
The unseen factor that in the end made all the difference
was the lack of depth in his faith in God. Right from the
beginning his faith had been a pale reflection of
Abraham's. He lived off Abraham's faith. He lived off
Abraham's blessings. He put up with Abraham's
problems for a time. But, for all his closeness to a man of
faith, he never seems to have gone beyond a shallow
experience of God for himself. Children or parents of
Christians can so easily be like him. For a time they go
along with everything as part of the overall set-up, but
they never make the faith of their parents or the faith of
their children a determining factor in their lives and
decisions. So they have no spiritual resources on which
to draw.

The result for Lot was that *he chose as the natural man
chooses – for himself.* 'So Lot chose for himself the whole
plain of the Jordan and set out towards the east' (Genesis
13:11). He apparently made a fairly quick choice on the
basis of obvious, outward and first impressions. He
'looked up and saw that the whole plain of Jordan was
well watered, like the garden of the Lord . . .' (Genesis
13:10). As a cattle man he felt that he did not need to
look twice. Good pasture was the prime criterion, and
here it was. Why make any further enquiries? Why
postpone a decision? Nevertheless, he made a bad

decision, for the conditions that he saw before him were only temporary and, while he could not be blamed for not knowing the future, there were other factors that he should have taken into account. What he saw was 'before the Lord destroyed Sodom and Gomorrah' (v. 10), but the moral state of those cities even then constituted a warning against becoming involved with them.

We can so easily make important decisions on temporary grounds. I remember boys working in a factory where I was employed, who gave up the chance of a good apprenticeship to a skilled trade because they could earn a few pounds more as errand boys in shops. Nothing could persuade them to think in longer terms. We can understand their immaturity and therefore their inability to see further ahead, yet we sometimes make far more serious decisions on the spur of the moment, without thinking long-term, much less in the eternal dimension. A hasty marriage for a moment's infatuation, a morally doubtful job for a bit more money, a move into a new area without discovering what it is really like, have caused havoc in the long run.

In making his decision, Lot does not seem to have considered his uncle at all. He knew what was good for himself and took it. And, as we have seen already, he *left out the moral and spiritual dimensions altogether*. These are the ones that make all the difference. They certainly did in Lot's case. He not only moved down to the valley, but he 'lived among the cities of the plain and pitched his tents near Sodom' (Genesis 13:12). He was too weak to resist the pull of the city lights and found himself sucked into the prevailing culture, even if he never became entirely a part of it. He certainly lost all power of affecting his contemporaries for good and eventually

had to run away from Sodom leaving everything
behind. Just as Abraham's faith influenced his family for
good, so Lot's decision to identify with Sodom affected
his family, too. His daughters finished up copying the
morals of the town and seducing their own drunken
father. Lot took no counsel and prayed no prayer. Who
needs to pray about such an obviously good piece of real
estate as the Jordan valley? He grabbed it and lost it,
and with it his integrity, his influence and his family.
Before we decide to move anywhere, we do well to
research the neighbourhood first and to take into full
account the prevailing moral tone, the spiritual
fellowship to be found there and the likely effect on
our family. That calls for real thought and constant
prayer.

We come back to the family upset that led to these
momentous results for both Abraham and Lot. One
ended up a bigger man for his pains. The other finished
on the scrap heap. Big doors turn on small hinges and we
may learn from their example how to cope with conflict
and how not to cope with choice. The battle began
because of a slowly changing situation that brought new
forces into play, and the age difference between the men
and their outlooks on life added complications. We do
well to ask ourselves what are the real causes of our
quarrels and what are the added ingredients. Then we
shall the better be able to come up with some solutions.
Abraham seized on a spiritual principle that provided a
framework for thinking. He recognized the realities that
he could not ignore and dealt with them through plain
common sense, but in doing so he showed a gracious
generosity of spirit that could not fail to impress itself on
Lot. Few of us would have been half as generous in a like
situation, but at this point his real living faith in God
made all the difference and enabled him to rise to new

heights of openness. He could afford to be generous if his inheritance was safe in the hands of God. So he took the initiative, offered the choice to Lot and opened himself to the risk of losing everything. In fact he lost nothing, grew in stature, and learnt as the days went on that God really does honour His promises if we will only trust Him. Lot, on the other hand, could only see his own future limited by this life and therefore demanding that he grasp every opportunity to better his own prospects. Abraham's faith enabled him to open his hand and let go, while Lot's limited outlook made him clutch tightly to everything he had. In life we have here the fundamental difference between faith and unbelief.

6

Faith's widening vision

Faith survives confrontations and grows in the course of them. But we take a battering in the process. At the end of it all those lingering doubts whether we have done the right thing remain. Supposing we had handled the quarrel differently, could we have saved the relationship? What if the other person comes to grief because of the choice he made at our request? Supposing we come out at the losing end after all? Maybe we should have handled it better. And so we go on and on, looking down at our feet and shuffling to and fro in agonies of questioning.

The Lord came to Abraham at the end of the crisis over Lot and brought him the sound advice: 'Lift up your eyes . . . and look' (Genesis 13:14). He needed to see where he was. He needed to take the long view. He needed the refreshment of distant horizons and their accompanying sense of release from prison. He needed to be able to take long deep breaths. The wide open spaces bring a sense of psychological relief. The prisoner sighs for a sight of something more than the handkerchief of sky that is all his cell provides for vision.

The Lord was doing more than giving Abraham a psychological lift. He was renewing again His first promise, and adding something more by way of detail.

Previously He had said He would give 'this land' in which he was living to Abraham's descendants (Genesis 12:7). Now He told him that those descendants would be 'like the dust of the earth, so that if anyone could count the dust, then your offspring could be counted' (Genesis 13:16). At this point Abraham had no descendants and the best part of the land had just gone to Lot. It was just then that the Lord called Abraham to take the big view and look in every direction, for everything he saw would one day become his. He had lost nothing by his generosity and had everything to look forward to. Tempted to look down, he was compelled to look up, see what was his and move on in faith.

The Scriptures apply this message to Christians again and again. God knows our capacity for looking at the pavement. After a period of conflict or testing He comes to enable us to take a fresh look at the heights and depths, lengths and breadths of our salvation. We know about them in the back of our minds, but God has to tell us to lift our eyes off the immediate circumstances and deliberately to contemplate what is in store for us. Our Father is Lord of the universe. 'God . . . has blessed us in the heavenly realms with every spiritual blessing in Christ' (Ephesians 1:3). 'No eye has seen, no ear has heard, no mind has conceived what God has prepared for those who love Him' (1 Corinthians 2:9). We need to take the eternal view. Then the incidents of time fall into perspective. Being the finite creatures we are, we cannot take in the full scope of God's plans for us in one glance. Now we focus on this facet, and then we focus on that one, but sometimes we need to take the broad view and let our breath be taken by the sheer overwhelming scope of it. So, after a difficult personal encounter, when our hearts are racked with doubts whether we have been too

soft or too hard, we need to hear God telling us to raise
our sights, take our eyes off the problem and have a fresh
look at the broad perspective.

Sometimes we need to look up in the plain physical
sense, as much as in the spiritual one. In a crowded
world where the multitudes of people press in upon us,
and a constant barrage of noise and information assaults
us from the press, television and radio, occasionally we
need to get away and look up and out. Otherwise we
may be pushed into a prison where the walls crush in
upon us and our programme dominates our personality.
We become stale and jaded and hard to live with. Then
we need to hear the Lord, or maybe some friend, saying,
'Lift up your eyes and look.' Even a glance at the sky can
work wonders. Or a look at the skyline of our own home
town can bring a new perspective that we never see
when our eyes are glued to the shop-windows or the
traffic. We may even need to heed the exhortation of the
hymn to 'lift up your eyes to the quiet hills', if there are
any around. Then the strident voices of materialism fall
silent and we begin to feel, as we say we believe, that
man's life does not consist in the abundance of things
which he possesses.

When Abraham looked in the four directions that
day, he was told to enter in not only to the scenery, but
to the excitement of partaking in a movement of history
that was to populate that scenery with the children of
God. He was not just looking at dust, but destiny.
Through all the region in his sight his descendants
would live and work and bring the earth to fruitfulness
under the plough. Not only was the view so much
greater than himself, but a fulfilment in a people
stretched forward down the reaches of history.

We, too, are invited by the Lord Himself to share in
that excitement and in the fulfilment of the destiny of
the people of God. But we must start to look up if we are
to see that. Jesus put it this way, 'Do you not say, "Four
months more and then the harvest"? I tell you, open
your eyes [or, in the more familiar words, Lift up your
eyes,] and look at the fields! They are ripe for harvest'
(John 4:35). The disciples were looking down and
worried about the meal they had just bought and they
were somewhat frustrated by the Samaritan woman
who had kept them from it. Jesus told them to stop
worrying, take their eyes off their dinner plates and look
at the people who even then were beginning to come out
to Him from Sychar. The disciples were bogged down in
things and Jesus was thrilled with people. He wanted
them to enter in with Him to the joy of seeing men and
women reconciled to God and finding satisfaction in
their new relationship. He wanted the disciples to find
their meat and drink, their whole sustenance in seeing
the people of Sychar entering the kingdom of God. 'My
food,' He said by way of example, 'is to do the will of him
who sent me and to finish his work' (John 4:34).

All we need to do to begin to see God's harvest among
people is to look over the garden fence. There we may
well find men and women just as thirsty for the water of
life as the Samaritan woman and her townsmen and,
just as Abraham was promised spiritual as well as
physical children, so we can enter into the blessing of
spiritual parenthood by sharing our faith with members
of our own street or community. We just need to look up
and see them in a new way. But we are no more limited
to a narrow view than Abraham was.

Right across the world today God is reaping His
harvest. He has been doing it ever since that day when

Jesus sat on the well while His disciples went shopping. Unfortunately, His people still seem occupied with their groceries and dinners and miss out on the excitement of people coming out of the cities and villages of the world to believe in Christ and to swell the ranks of the people of God. If Abraham really is 'the father of us all' who share 'the faith of Abraham' (Romans 4:16), then these people are just a part of the fulfilment of the vision given to Abraham that 'I will make your offspring like the dust of the earth' (Genesis 13:16). When our eyes are on our shopping bags we do not see them. A small illustration of this trend is clear in the realm of literature. I am told on good authority that American bookstores will not stock most missionary books because they do not sell. Part of the blame no doubt lies with dull missionary writers, but to be fair to them, most people never even open the books. Ask your bookseller. He can sell any amount of books on demons, spiritual gifts, stories of personalities, sex and marriage, or how to cope with life and be successful. To sell a missionary book is an achievement. By and large we do not want to know. Our eyes need lifting up from material and personal preoccupations.

Yet the Lord told us to lift up our eyes and look, in order to stimulate and encourage us. We are not alone. However small our congregations, in some parts of the world people are flocking into the churches. In other parts people are beginning to trickle towards the Lord in as unpropitious circumstances as Samaria represented when He was on earth. 'Look,' He says, 'Get involved in this exciting movement of the Spirit across the world and play your part in the destiny of the people of God.' Abraham had nothing but a promise to go on in his day, but he believed God for a miracle. We have so much more to encourage us.

The sad thing is that while in my own country I find the church largely inward-looking and lacking a world-wide vision, I find Christians elsewhere awakening to the thrill of taking part in God's plan. Asian Christians are seeing that God has a place for them in mission, too, and we now rejoice in having in our own fellowship sixty fine fellow workers from places like Singapore, Malaysia, Japan, Hong Kong, Taiwan, the Philippines and Korea. Churches are taking up missionary budgets, sometimes of thousands of dollars. One Singaporean church fully supports its own missionary to Niger with the Sudan Interior Mission, and does it to the tune of £500 per month from a remarkably young congregation. There is a spirit of faith and optimism in those churches that God intends for all His people, but we keep our eyes solidly glued to our own domestic problems and miss out on the wider purposes of our God. People of faith cannot afford this restricted outlook. The field is the world. Lift up your eyes and look.

Abraham believed God when he looked across the land. Yet Abraham did not ever see the land become his and had to wait for a very long time for his first real descendant. That did not deter him. God said, 'Go, walk through the length and breadth of the land, for I am giving it to you' (Genesis 13:17). So when God said, 'Go', he went. Success is no criterion of obedience. Faith responds to the command of God. Sometimes we insist that if we do what God wants then He must come up with the answers right away. He does not necessarily do that. God wanted to encourage Abraham with the broad view, but He also expected from Abraham the continued walk that moved towards the goal, even when the goal never seemed to come any nearer. When we have persevered for years in prayer for someone and that person seems as far away from God as when we began, we must pray on. When we have claimed our workplace for the Lord and we believe He has put us there to see spiritual offspring fill that place, yet so far no one is the least bit interested, we must stay on. When we have sought to gain a victory in some sphere of our lives and we have failed again and again and we are tempted to give up and feel that God's promises just never will be fulfilled, we must hope on. The present lack of encouragement in no way limits the reality of the original vision. In God's time we shall see His fulfilment, though it may not be in the way that we expect. In the meantime God means us to go on.

Missionaries worked among the Lun Bawang people in Borneo for a long time. Eventually the government advised them to withdraw and to leave a people so corrupted to the penalties of their own debauchery. The war intervened and Christians from Indonesia crossed the border to share their faith with this downcast people. The Spirit of God came down upon them and eventually the government officials discovered that in the place of drunken bouts of several days duration, daily hymn-singing and worship characterized the tribe. No one expected God to reach the Lun Bawang from another direction, but what does it matter whom He uses when people are changed and brought to life? What did matter was that people from the West and people from Indonesia both heard the command of God to go and walk through the land, and they went. Eventually the Lord did what He had planned.

Here once again we see something of the paradox of faith. On the one hand the Lord showed Abraham the broad sweep of His plans and lifted his spirits above any lingering uncertainties from the confrontation with Lot. On the other hand God called him to go on in obedience with the broad sweep of God's purpose still imprinted on his brain even as he moved from place to place in his daily life. Faith looks up and faith presses on. Faith pierces the veil between what is to be and what is, and faith walks the road of daily obedience.

7

Faith and politics

Russia walks into Afghanistan! What has that to do with me? Boycott the Moscow Olympics! Why should sport be dragged into politics? If only other people would leave us alone! Let us keep religion and politics separate. Faith is a personal thing. Do not carry it into the market-place to get trodden underfoot. Politics are a dirty game and war is worse. Leave other people to sort out their own problems. We have enough of our own.

How much easier life would be if we really could opt out of the events that shatter the peace of our world! Yet Jesus warned us that there would be wars and rumours of wars and that our hearts were not to be troubled. He did not promise freedom from political unrest and disturbance and He sometimes uses such things to strengthen and to test the faith that we have. Abraham found that out, too, when he learnt that his nephew Lot was again in trouble.

At the beginning of chapter 14 of Genesis we find Lot caught up in a war of the kings, and himself and his family taken as prisoners of war. Other eyes than his had been cast upon the well-watered plains of Jordan, and those other eyes were backed by armed forces. Too late he began to realize that all that glitters is not gold.

Abraham, of course, could easily have washed his

hands of him. 'He has made his bed, let him lie on it.'
But the man or woman of faith cannot do that. God did
not do it to humanity in its sin. God became personally
involved. Abraham had to do the same. Someone
escaped the catastrophe and came and told Abraham,
and 'when Abram heard that his relative had been
·taken captive, he called out the 318 trained men born in
his household.' Relationship counted, even if the
particular relation had landed himself in trouble by his
own choice.

Relationships within the human family should still
count as much. Within the people of God, members of
His family, they should count still more. Maybe the
young person who was warned about certain friends is
now hopelessly caught in the drug scene. Maybe the girl
married that fellow when everyone except herself could
see that it would end in disaster. We still have to get
involved, and sometimes to pick up the pieces. Maybe
the government in Kampuchea was terribly corrupt
and that particular regime deserved to disappear, and
maybe the people trusted the wrong government to take
its place, but we cannot stand by and do nothing when a
whole nation is in danger of extinction. Believers, true
believers and nominal ones, are caught up in the general
tragedy. We cannot leave them to perish in refugee
camps without coming to their aid. Nowhere can
Christians stand on the touch-line and refuse to take
part in the action when other people are stripped of all
they possess, deprived of human rights, and held captive
by their enemies. The involvement of Jesus in the
incarnation and on the cross forbids us to sit still and
watch it happen. No more can we stand aside and do
nothing while men and women are taken as really
captive by Satan and bound in the chains of spiritism,

occultism, drugs, pornography, or even that
respectability that glosses over and hides the bondage of
sin. 'This is not your rest.' We have to be involved. That,
too, is a part of the life of faith.

Abraham had only three hundred and eighteen men
altogether. He could have pleaded the smallness of his
forces. We know, too, from secular history that
Chedorlaomer was no local chieftain and no man to be
trifled with. He was, moreover, the head at that
particular time of a confederacy of four kings that had
just beaten five others. Abraham had good reason for
keeping out of the quarrel. Interference looked strangely
like suicide. Why do it?

The man of faith reasons differently. His relative was
involved and that overrode all other considerations. He
owed it to Lot to help him and owing is at the root of
'ought'. When people are our brothers and sisters, and
especially when they are brothers and sisters in Christ,
we cannot let them suffer if it is in our power to do
something about it. The smallness of the resources
available has never really deterred true faith. The Lord
is on our side. 'There is a lad here,' is matched by the
power of Christ, and the five thousand find food. The
size of the army is not always the important factor in the
battle. Sometimes small is beautiful, as later on Gideon
found when the Lord sent most of his army home before
the battle began. Did not the great apostle say, 'When I
am weak, then I am strong'? Did Jesus not hang upon
the cross all alone? In situations like these we are
brought inexorably back to how real is our belief in God.
If He is truly existent and almighty, we need not fear to
take on the world. If He is just another idea that we
happen to have about the meaning of life, we shall be too
scared to do anything. Hudson Taylor's robust faith
coined the phrase: 'First it is impossible, then it is

difficult, then it is done.'

The sad fact today is that the small groups that make the biggest impact are usually anarchists, nihilists, terrorists or Communists. They wield an influence far beyond their numbers, while the church cowers in the corner bemoaning her poverty and paucity and planning the closure of her buildings and the reduction of her ministry, at least in some Western countries. In fact, even in those places the churches have far greater resources than the other groups. A loss of nerve is what makes them unable to use those forces. 'Blessed with every spiritual blessing in Christ' (Ephesians 1:3), the Christian church acts like a spiritual pauper. The problem does not lie in numbers or wealth, but in lack of living contact with the God who really *is*. We do not really believe what we say we believe, and when we are called to act on the belief without human props and assurances to help us we find ourselves unwilling to step out.

In becoming involved Abraham was not stupid. He thought about what he was doing and carefully planned his campaign. Lacking in strength, he needed to catch the enemy unawares. Surprise was his biggest advantage. A victorious army returning home does not expect a sudden counter-attack in the middle of the night from the same direction as the defeated forces of the enemy (Genesis 14:15). Night-time would also give the advantage of confusion. So Abraham split his meagre army and risked everything on a two-pronged assault that succeeded perfectly. The enemy fled in disarray and Abraham brought back all the goods that had been lost and rescued Lot and his family among the rest (Genesis 14:16).

Contrary to the slander of the world, walking by faith does not mean abandoning common sense or the use of

our minds. We are told to have transformed and
renewed minds (Romans 12:2) and to have minds ready
for energetic action (1 Peter 1:13), but we are not told to
stop thinking. The gospel, when truly understood,
enables a person to think in a valid way for the first time.
Until submission to God in Christ, people think of the
universe with the biggest piece of the jigsaw puzzle lost
or left out, so that their thinking can hardly be really
integrated. So Abraham was right to use his mind and
was not expected to launch a foolish frontal assault in
the name of faith. So, today, any approach to difficult
and dangerous activities must be carefully thought
through. In the early seventies, Phnom Penh was a
dangerous place in which to live. At times rockets
landed indiscriminately in the city every day. As we
were approaching the airport to land, a delightful
young Cambodian leaned across the aisle separating his
seat from mine and said, 'Are you not afraid to come to
our city? There is fighting just outside this airport every
night.' We had been invited to send missionaries to live
there. On what basis should we decide? As we were
thinking and praying over that invitation at our Central
Council meetings in Singapore a little later, a leading
Cambodian Christian suddenly arrived in the city to
plead the cause of his people. They were our kinsmen in
Christ. Could we fail to be involved? Yet we also had to
think through the implications of the dangerous
situation. Dare we send parents of young children, or
even married couples? Who could make the maximum
contribution in what might be a very short time? What
kind of work needed doing most? How were we to relate
best to the church and to C & M A, the mission that had
done the spadework there for nearly fifty years? How
would we keep in touch with workers there? How would

they receive money for supplies? What about the language problem? How about taking people from existing important commitments? We could not just rush in without thinking seriously about all of these matters.

For Abraham, too, involvement spelt danger. We can easily admire his courage and applaud his action, for we know what happened in the end, but he did not know what the result would be when he put his life on the line. But danger to life, limb or property never justified a believer in failing to get involved. On one occasion Hudson Taylor planned to set out for an area of China known to be very dangerous at the time, and his friends urged him to stay where he was in case he should be killed. Back came his reply immediately: 'We ought to lay down our lives for the brethren.' Every now and then, Christian workers have to do just that. Since the last war, in the membership of the OMF, two have been kidnapped and six have been shot and killed, together with a Christian businessman friend who risked his life to see for himself how brothers and sisters in Christ were faring. He could so easily have stayed at home. These people laid their lives on the line, not at the moment when someone pointed a gun at them, but at the moment when they committed themselves to a course of action that had that end result. Faced with death they had no choice. Someone else pulled the trigger. The real crunch comes when we commit ourselves to obedience, wherever that may lead, and that is something required of every Christian wherever he or she lives. Indeed, terrible as murder and sudden death may be to face at the final moment, many people go on facing killing circumstances day after day that require just as much courage to encounter. Continuing a ministry in the

inner-city areas of New York or London, Sydney or
Tokyo when everything within you cries out, 'I want
out,' is just as demanding. But we cannot opt out. We
have a responsibility to our kinsmen. Someone has to act
for them, for they are held captive and are unable to
help themselves.

The sad thing is that, as we look at a world where
refugees are more numerous than ever before, where
hunger and poverty dog the lives of vast numbers of
people, and where millions still have no chance to hear
of the deliverance from inner bondage available in
Christ, the involvement of many Christians is limited to
watching the tragedy played out on their television
screens, or to the occasional donation. By and large the
church with all its resources sleeps on while the people
who get involved are the terrorists, the nihilists, the
Communists and others with a faith sufficiently
integrated with their daily lives to impel them to
attempt to take over our world.

Abraham brought his campaign to a successful
conclusion, but as far as benefit to himself is concerned,
he had nothing to show for it. His sole reward, humanly
speaking, lay in seeing other people set free and restored
to a full life once again. Yet it is said of the Messiah in
Isaiah 53 that He shall see of the travail of His soul and
be satisfied. What a satisfaction that is! One shattered
life put together again, one home restored to peace and
love, one misfit found a place, can make up for all the
labour.

Certainly involvement is not materially enriching.
Abraham received nothing financial as a result of his
efforts. In fact, he probably faced quite a big bill for
expenses. So, today, the Christian worker rarely finishes
active life with anything like enough even to put down

as a deposit on a house, let alone buy one, no capital saved and little to pass on to the family. Being human, a person finds it difficult to listen to a friend debating his serious problem whether to buy a third car in the family for his daughter or whether to buy a boat. But when the day is done, the real reward is still there in human lives changed and in the effects that reach beyond the time when both boat and car lie rotting and eternity stretches beyond the sunset in the place where human values at last begin to count. In any case, whatever the result and whatever the cost, we have no choice. Men and women of faith must get involved.

Fundamentally, involvement is a question of obedience. Obedience flows from relationship with both God and man. The result of obedience in terms of material loss or gain is neither here nor there. Cold hard obedience is out of favour in a generation that likes to be high on feeling, but it may just be the very aspect of the Christian life that could make all the difference.

Just as Abraham was about to close his books on the whole incident, someone met him to impart a fresh challenge at the moment of victory. Melchizedek, king of Salem, 'priest of God Most High' (Genesis 14:17,18) came out to bless him. At the same time he reminded Abraham that the victory of his puny forces against the mighty armies of the enemy did not really belong to Abraham, but to the God who actively rules the universe (Genesis 14:19,20). The expedition could easily have ended in disaster. Yet God had honoured Abraham's obedience and delivered his enemies into his hand. Victory was not a time for boasting, but for humble and thankful acknowledgement of the grace of God. The glory of the occasion belonged to Him. Abraham responded by accepting the blessing, giving a

tenth of his own goods by way of thanksgiving, and
refusing to benefit in any way personally from his
victory. He told the kings that he wanted no reward, but
at the same time he was careful not to deny his allies
their freedom to accept a share of the spoils.

A principle shines through this incident that might
well be heeded by our publicity-conscious generation of
Christians. Too often the glory of some campaign or
series of meetings goes to the organizers, or the preacher,
or the evangelist. I have known one of the many world
conferences that afflict the Christian world today
acclaimed as 'historic' before it was even held. Afraid
that what we are doing may find no place in history, we
can seek to give it a place it does not deserve. Speakers
are applauded for the length of their travels and the size
of their congregations in this place or that, and the little
phrase at the end: 'And to God be all the glory' is meant
to justify it all. By that stage there is nothing left.

We all face the temptation after the event to forget
our trembling knees and butterfly stomachs and to bask
in the success of the effort. If every time we saw a victory
we could humbly accept the blessing as from God, and
even more if we felt obliged to give a tithe of our income
at that point to demonstrate that we are not just
mouthing words, we might not make such exaggerated
claims for our ministry. The glory would then be seen
clearly as going to God. Jesus told us that at the end of
the day all we could really claim is that, 'We are
unworthy servants; we have only done our duty' (Luke
17:10).

8

Faith looks upward and forward

'Lord, I really feel in need of some encouragement. I have been going on for some time now and really I do not have very much to show for it. I know that faith is the substance of things unseen, but sometimes I really would like to see something. You have made me great promises, but a person cannot live on promises all his life. I have become involved in some difficult circumstances because of the family of God and, quite frankly, I am scared what is going to result. I feel exposed and I feel in need of reassurance. I do believe, and I do trust You, but can I not receive some token, some practical indication that I am not building castles in the air?'

Does that sound too much like grumbling? Surely the spiritual man or woman will not talk to God like that. Well, Abraham did, and we think none the worse of him for doing so. He, like us, was human, and his natural longings to see the son who had been promised to him sometimes came out on top. The concept of the life of faith as one in which we go sailing calmly along, free of pressures and disappointments and never feeling like complaining, is not a biblical one. Jesus told His disciples that they would have to die daily, and dying never will be a pleasant experience. The resurrection that lies beyond the dying is another matter, but the dying has to be gone through first. Problems, trials and agonizing decisions have to be faced by everyone. The difference for the people of faith is that they know that the important point is not steering clear of trouble, but facing it in the strength of God and proving His power in the middle of it. 'Consider it pure joy, my brothers,' says James, 'whenever you face trials of many kinds, because you know that the testing of your faith develops perseverance.' The athlete who would win has to push his muscles to the limit, and that cannot be done without aches and pains.

Abraham had involved himself in Lot's problem during the war in which the latter was taken captive and he had emerged victorious. Yet he then had second thoughts. Kings do not take kindly to being robbed of the spoils of war. Once the defeated kings realized how small were the forces that had routed them they could very easily be back for their revenge. The exposure that Abraham faced therefore was not over when the battle was won. He had then to live in a state of apprehension about a possible counter-attack. We have already seen how he refused to take any remuneration for his services, wanting to be able to give the glory only to God who in truth had given him the victory. So all he had left was an anxious mind. Was obedience really worth it?

God knew Abraham's need. He appeared to him in a vision and said, 'Do not be afraid, Abram. I am your shield, your very great reward' (Genesis 15:1). Abraham had a number of experiences in his life when God came to him afresh with new assurances and when His presence was particularly meaningful. Each time the assurance perfectly met the need. Between those appearances the days went by in a succession of small acts of obedience and worship, with nothing spectacular to report. Yet on at least four occasions the special manifestation marked a new milestone in Abraham's experience.

God still meets the needs of His children in similar ways. Sometimes the new experience is as vivid as a vision. Sometimes it is hard to put it into words, but God is there, so close that it is as though He could be touched and the heart feels strangely warmed, as John Wesley once felt. Some people have crystallized experiences that have been particularly vivid in their own lives and, in going to the Scriptures to explain them, have come up with a formula that they then try to apply universally. Some say that it is through an experience of 'entire sanctification'. Some say that it is 'the rest of faith'. 'Let go and let God,' is their advice. Others tell us that we must learn to be 'crucified with Christ'. More recently the seeking of the 'baptism in the Spirit' has been advocated as something to be sought.

The underlying truth that comes to me is that God's Spirit is sovereign and He deals with people as He wills. I do not doubt any of the experiences of these my brethren, but each seems to be explaining God's sovereign grace in terms of the particular way in which it has come to him or her. The danger is that we can stereotype the work of the Spirit of God, argue with each other over different theories and finish up further from God than when we began. Do we have to limit God's blessings to two? As we have seen, Abraham seems to have had four distinct advances in his spiritual life. Should we be content with two? If we are pressing on to know the Lord more and more, can we not leave with Him and to His initiative the times when He will draw especially near? We do not have to urge others to experience the manifold grace of God in exactly the same way that we do. The circumcision party in the early church made that mistake. While every experience must be tested by, and conform to, the teaching of the Word of God, that does not mean that we can then elevate our own experience to a norm, however scriptural it is. Apart from the basic doctrines and fundamental truths which are essential to salvation, a wide variety of Christian experience receives justification from Scripture. To insist that everyone has the same experience in the same order is to limit the Spirit of God, put people into a mould and cause controversy and even division.

I remember a leading national Christian in Sarawak whom God used very much during a time of revival, to avoid the twin dangers of quenching the Spirit or splitting the church. He told us of his experience when all around him God was dealing with people in remarkable ways. Some were struck down under conviction of sin. Others had power to discern the specific sins of other people and to sense who it was whose way of living was troubling the purity of the church. Through it all the leader was longing to be part of the blessing. 'Lord, do not pass me by,' was his prayer. But then the Lord brought peace to his heart and showed him that provided he was sincerely wanting the very best and seeking to serve Christ in every way, he did not have to have the same experience as his brethren. Their need was one and his was another. No one who knows that man doubts that he is a man full of the Spirit of God. His wisdom, a real gift of the Spirit, saved those churches from many a serious division. Yet he himself at that time had no new startling experience.

Abraham did not seek this new experience that he had. God came to him and gave it. Indeed we find right through his life that God was always taking the initiative. God has always done so, and still does. He it was who decided that the world should exist at all and that we as individuals should have a part in it. He it was who sent His only begotten Son to save us from our sins. He it was who revealed Himself to us as a race and as individuals in the first place. Can we not rest content that 'He who did not spare his own Son, but gave him up for us all—how will he not also, along with him, graciously give us all things?' (Romans 8:32.) I am not suggesting that spiritual laziness will be rewarded. Abraham went on in regular worship and obedience. The Lord came to him when he was ready to receive something more. Faith is ready to trust God to do just that.

The place of feelings in the Christian life has always been difficult to define. Believers are human and emotion is a part of humanity. Feelings are not faith, but they do affect our enjoyment of faith and our ability to see things in perspective. Faith that grits its teeth and staggers through life solely on the basis of the bare word with never any feeling at all is more Stoic than Christian. Yet sometimes faith has to manage without feelings. Then God comes again with a warmth that renews the glow in our hearts and we know the joy of sensation. At such times we can sense the same comfort that came to Abraham when God began by saying to him, 'Do not be afraid.'

As usual, God's message to Abraham fitted his need like a glove. He told him not to be afraid of attack because God was his shield, and not to be afraid of loss because God was his reward. Every assault on the

servant of God had of necessity to get past his shield, and
if that shield was the infinite and almighty God, then he
had no cause for fear. His visible forces were meagre, his
invisible forces dominant. Similarly, his refusal of the
trinkets offered by the grateful kings might seem to
deprive him of any benefit from his action, but if God
was really his reward, there was nothing that he could
need. Abraham knew enough of the reality of God at
that stage to trust Him with his safety and with his
possessions. Modern man finds that very hard to do.
Philosophy has been saying for nearly two hundred
years that nothing beyond the reach of man's five senses
can possibly be known in a valid way. Only the material
can be real. Few men may know the philosophy, but by
now it has seeped through to the popular level and is all
the more insidious for not being formulated mentally. It
is just taken for granted. Therefore, to let go of your
possessions and trust a God you cannot see is to modern
man the height of stupidity. Even Christians find it hard
to do. Only when we have refused the world's
enrichment and divorced ourselves from the world's
security, do we arrive at the place where we can prove
God's reality and know for sure that He is able both to
guard and to reward.

What God is really saying here is that we can never
lose out by obedience. God Himself is greater than any
gift and safer than any shelter. He is our shield in every
battle and our reward in every share-out. We do not
have to go around grabbing at everything in case we lose
it, when we have a God like that. Yet we are a
calculating and security-minded generation, taught to
think for ourselves and assuming that we always think
rightly. So we find it easy to lean on our own
understanding and hard to 'trust in the Lord with all

your heart' (Proverbs 3:5). Jesus expressed His confidence in His Father's protection when He said to Pilate, 'You would have no power over me if it were not given to you from above' (John 19:11). Every appearance spoke to the contrary, but behind the seen lay the great Unseen dictating the limits of every action. When this world of the unseen is alive to us we can rise above the circumstances that otherwise would lead us to despair. Our world is growing sick of materialism, and the multiplication of religions and cults shows a return to seeking something beyond the seen. Here is the great opportunity for those who know indeed that God Himself is our protection in every hostile environment, and our enrichment in the midst of materialism. The world wants a new way, but seldom sees it demonstrated by God's people.

Despite God's reassurance, Abraham still had a complaint to make, and he made it honestly. He said, 'O Sovereign Lord, what can you give me since I remain childless and the one who will inherit my estate is Eliezer of Damascus?' He put it even more specifically: 'You have given me no children; so a servant in my household will be my heir.' He did not doubt the sovereign reign of God. But that was a part of the problem. If God really was the Ruler of all, why did He not give Abraham the one thing that he wanted above everything else? The promise of a son rang a little hollow when a foreigner was the only possible heir he could see. Here was the deep cry of a human heart. Abraham had come to the land with promises. He still only had promises. His patience was wearing thin and so he said, 'You have given me no children.' Many a person can echo Abraham's heart-cry, whether it be for a child, or a husband, or a healing, or a hope.

Abraham was a man of faith. He was also made of flesh and blood and, like many people of faith since that time, he reached the point where his patience was stretched to the limit. 'I want to see something. I want to see it now.' Weary of waiting, we find the assurance of God's unseen presence is not enough. We long for something else, maybe even something we believe God promised to give. So we cry out in complaint that God has withheld the one blessing that is our heart's desire, and we add a guilty conscience to our problems because we feel we should not complain. We are in good company. Abraham, the friend of God, the ideal man of faith, complained, too. And the Lord understood.

When you stop to think about it, we do say some amazing things to God, and often choose the most inopportune time. The Lord had just promised to Abraham an everlasting security and an eternal provision. He had spoken in terms like those of Romans 8:28-39 of the impossibility of anything separating him from His love. Yet, like a child with a fixation about one particular toy, he seizes upon the one thing he does not have and complains about that. Like the child, he loses sight of all the wonderful things provided already. Like the human father, the Heavenly Father understands.

The Lord's answer has been described by the Rev. Alan Stibbs in these terms: 'If Abraham was not satisfied, neither was God. The one born in his house was not fit to be his heir. God had better plans than that. Sometimes we foolishly assume that the Lord is satisfied with less than we are. But he is not. He is more patient than we are about bringing it to completion and providing everything necessary on the way. But in the process He is bringing many sons to glory, including ourselves, and His education of those sons includes lessons of patience, faith and obedience.'

So the Lord took Abraham outside for an object lesson (Genesis 15:5). '"Look up at the heavens and count the stars—if indeed you can count them." Then he said to him, "So shall your offspring be."' Sometimes a bit of star-gazing can do us good. There we see the majesty of space, the immensity of infinity, the perspective of size and distance and the generosity of creation. God was saying to Abraham, 'Think big. I do. Look at the results of My creative activity. Once there was nothing. Now there is unsearchable, unlimited magnitude and multiplicity. See what I brought from nothing. Look beyond the covers of your tiny tent, the confined corners of your little world and out into the immensity of space. You will see how small you are, but you will also see how great I am, for I made them all. Am I really incapable of giving you a son born naturally?' God could have then spoken to Abraham about the one son he was to have, but instead He took him out to look down the years to people as numerous as the stars, and all Abraham's descendants.

We know far more about the immensity and complexity of space than Abraham did. Unfortunately, modern man, in learning something of how small he is in relation to the size of the universe, has drawn the wrong conclusion that he cannot possibly count at all. Instead of seeing the majesty of the God who made it all and bowing down in worship, he has concluded that such a universe or succession of universes is too big for even God to have made. It must have all been an accident. But God did make it and, when we realize that, we begin to see how laughable it is to think that He cannot cope with our special problems. Moreover, we begin to think big as He does. We begin to think in world-wide terms.

We look at impenetrable Islam and see God bringing a great harvest from it. We see Him who multiplied the stars calling out churches from Communist states. We see the crowds of the world as in His sight, and we begin to see our own difficulties and impossibilities in perspective.

We have allowed militant rationalism to rob us of the lessons of the universe. We live in God's creation. He makes something out of nothing. He brings forth fruit in old age. We only have to look at the stars and see. Abraham, the old man, became the father of a nation as numerous as those stars. Unfortunately for many of us, the lights of the modern towns and cities in which we live obscure and blot out the gentle shining of the stars. We cannot see God's handiwork because our own has filled the horizon. I count it a great privilege to have been able to go out into the tropical countryside at night and see the breath-taking panorama that shines down at you in untarnished glory. The longer you look, the more you see. The visual impression is underlined by the chorus of innumerable crickets, scissor grinders, and other choristers of the insect world singing the creative power of the Lord. And then you can almost hear God's still small voice: 'So shall your offspring be.'

Just at this point in the story we read, in Genesis 15:6, words that have rung down the centuries: 'Abram believed the Lord, and he credited it to him as righteousness.' Here we have the first statement of the truth of justification by faith. Abraham, the old man, the good-as-dead man, has come to realize that he is incapable of producing life himself. He has tried and failed. Spiritually the sinner has to be brought to the same conclusion before he or she can hope to live. We have no life in ourselves and because of what we are we are totally incapable of producing any. Then for Abraham God came along with a promise of life entirely dissociated from merit or human action and, indeed, at the very place where man was closest to despair. Abraham believed that promise and in doing so abandoned all self-centred attempts to provide his own answer. That is what is at the centre of justification by faith. The root of Adam's sin had been a do-it-yourself mentality that sought independence of the Creator on the basis of man knowing the difference between right and wrong and being perfectly capable of making right decisions. This contradicted the whole position of man as a creature and exalted him to a position of equality with God as an independent autonomous being. Abraham had come to realize that there was no future that way. He was a creature and had to behave as one, and therefore he consciously submitted his will to God and declared his readiness to trust Him as the Creator to produce the life that was needed. God accepted that humble attitude of complete trust as the 'right' relationship to Him.

We now know that there is more to justification by faith than just that, for the problem of the alienation caused by sin had to be dealt with effectively by the death of Jesus Christ, the sinless One, on the cross. We also know that Jesus Christ is the 'offspring' that God ultimately had in mind as the One through whom the whole world would be blessed.

From the human side we have to take the same position that Abraham took. 'Lord, I cannot do anything to produce that life that I need. I am utterly dependent upon You to do it. If You tell me that Jesus died for my sin and took my place upon the cross I will accept Your word as true. If You tell me that I must trust

Him absolutely and commit my life to Him and that then You will accept me as in right relationship with Yourself, then I will gladly abandon my own self-effort and accept as a creature what You have done. And then, Lord, I must go and live for You, not in order to be accepted, but because I am accepted and I want to show my love.' That is justification by faith.

We began this chapter in something of a complaining mood. The heart was crying out for some assurance when the going was tough and everything seemed to rely on things unseen. We finish it with the assurance that comes both from creation and from the cross. God not only tells us that He is our shield in every struggle and our reward in every distribution, but that in His creation and in Jesus' cross lie visible assurances that God has already brought something out of nothing and life out of death. Can we not trust Him to bring us the warmth of feeling and new revelations of love in His own good time?

9

Faith under depression

'A Christian should never be depressed.' Some would even say a Christian should never be sick. They are out of touch with reality. Christians are human beings and have nerves and emotions just like everyone else, and nothing in Scripture indicates that they will avoid the common afflictions of human life. Not, of course, that everyone has to become depressed, or that all of us go through exactly the same feelings, but to suggest that there is something lacking in the depressed person is to misunderstand him or her cruelly. Many of the mystics of the Middle Ages spoke of the 'dark night of the soul', and they were not lacking in spiritual determination, discipline and prayer. Abraham went through a time of deep darkness, a time when he must have wondered if it would ever end, and whether he would ever see the light at the end of the tunnel. Interestingly, too, this experience immediately followed a spiritual 'high' when God had brought fresh assurance to him. In fact, the depression seems almost directly related to a renewed dedication and commitment to God that followed the new assurance. Knowing the facts of spiritual warfare, we should not really be surprised at that. It is often those who have never gone beyond the shallow stages of Christian living who tell us confidently that depression holds no place in the life of the believer. Satan does not have to bother with those whose lives are little threat to his kingdom. He wrestles with the ones whose commitment takes them out into the deep.

Let us look more closely into Abraham's experience. Genesis 15:7 comes immediately after the acceptance by God of Abraham's complete trust in His power and wisdom to supply the son whom Abraham was incapable of producing. At once Abraham was faced with the tension that every believer faces between the 'now' and the 'not yet'. The Lord said to him, 'I am the Lord, who brought you out of Ur of the Chaldeans to give you this land to take possession of it.' That was the 'not yet', the promise of things to come. But Abraham said, 'O Sovereign Lord, how can I know that I will gain possession of it?' That was the 'now' in a land where the Canaanites were much in evidence and in control of the government. Abraham could see that the Lord intended to fulfil His promise, but so much around him reminded him that there was a very long way to go. Every believer knows that tension, which for Christians is expressed in the truth of the kingdom of God which is the rule of God now and among His people, but which is 'not yet' manifested over the whole world. Sometimes it is hard to believe that the promised day will ever come. The forces of evil seem to have plenty of say in governing the world, and the kingdom of God seems to be confined to a few tents here and there, scattered across a hostile countryside.

We may then want to cry out of the depth of our hearts with Abraham, 'How am I to *know* that I shall possess it?' Coming so soon after Abraham's reaction of faith to the Lord's lesson from the stars, this cry sounds like a reversion to doubt. On the other hand, we can also

look at it from the point of view that deeper faith is not
content with shallow assurance. The person who has
begun to taste the depths that are possible in
relationship with God wants to go deeper in every
direction. Therefore depth, and not doubt, may be the
source of the cry. At the same time, honestly expressed
doubt has its own part to play in the expression of true
faith, for faith that is never assailed by doubt probably
has little depth.

Abraham asked for a new assurance. God in turn
asked for a renewed commitment and for the
presentation of a sacrifice as the basis of a visible
covenant agreement between Himself and His servant.
When we ask the Lord for more we cannot expect to
receive without in turn giving more of ourselves. The
Lord called for the offering of a three-year-old heifer,
goat and ram, and of a turtle-dove and pigeon.
Abraham brought them, cut them in two and arranged
the halves opposite each other, except in the case of the
birds. Solemn agreements were often sealed in this way
by the two parties passing between the pieces in token
that they were staking their lives on their commitment
to the outcome. So in Hebrew the language used for
making a covenant is to 'cut' it. Abraham had then done
his part.

Time went on and nothing happened. Abraham
found himself keeping the birds of prey off the carcasses
and it kept him busy all day. Still nothing happened. As
the relentless sun at last went down and the birds
stopped their foraging, Abraham fell asleep, probably
exhausted. Then in the depths of his sleep depression
dark and lowering struck him. The Bible describes it as a
'thick and dreadful darkness' that came over him. He
heard the Lord speaking of the future of his people in a

country not their own, where slavery and mistreatment were to come to them. The horrors of servitude destroyed any peace in his sleep and left him more exhausted than when he had begun. Still there was no new assurance.

Have you ever felt as Abraham felt that day? Seeking new assurance and longing perhaps for a deeper relationship with God, you have prepared the sacrifice and laid everything in order on the altar of your heart. You have then had to defend the offering from the attacking hordes of doubt and disbelief, criticism and mockery, until, exhausted with anticipation, you have dropped wearily to sleep. And through it all nothing has happened. The heavens remain like brass and God seems to have left His world. Where is the fire from heaven? Why make the offering if nothing happens? Obedience is met by silence. Everything has been done and nothing has happened.

Part of our problem in the twentieth century is our 'instant' mentality. Instant coffee, instant meals, instant entertainment—all school us to think in instant terms. Moreover, evangelical Christians in particular have seized upon formulae and clichés that we are told will always work. So our bookshops are full of simple answers to complicated problems. We are assured that if we only do A, B and C then D, E and F are bound to follow. We forget we are dealing with God. Having lost most of our sense of awe and majesty in a world where any form of distinction is anathema, we are in danger of slipping into a push-button mentality. If we do this, then God is bound to do that. But the Lord is not bound and will not be bound by men. He is God. Certainly He has given us principles to follow that are valid for all time. Equally certainly He keeps His promises, but He is not bound to

act either in the way we expect or at the time that we
hope He will. He is the Lord. He is not at our beck and
call; we are at His. So we may fulfil all the conditions
and still have to wait for His time.

Abraham could not expect the fulfilment of God's
promises until Israel had grown into a people, been
brought to a stage where they were ready to respond to
the call to leave Egypt, and were sufficiently unhappy
there to be only too glad to launch out on the exodus. In
other words, God's purposes for Abraham involved the
lives of many other people besides his own. We are not
the only people to be taken into account in God's
dealings with men and women. Sometimes what we
long for Him to do in us or for us is dependent upon His
being able to bring someone else to a place where they
can fit into the plan, and that takes time. So we have to
wait as Abraham had to wait.

Weary with waiting, Abraham slept and experienced
a great depression. 'Hope deferred,' says the proverb,
'makes the heart sick.' Sick hearts are often tired hearts
and depression can easily come to them. Looking for
fire, Abraham found frustration and darkness. Slavery
was coming. Oppression was coming and Abraham was
learning that 'we must go through many hardships to
enter the kingdom of God' (Acts 14:22).

The chord of suffering is largely absent from the music
of Christian living and teaching in the West today. We
live surrounded by a world bent on pleasure, security,
entertainment and self-fulfilment and the jolt that
suffering introduces into that world is largely
unacceptable. Even in the Christian sphere we promise
new believers freedom from problems, a spring in their
step, a smile on their face. We tell them to smile because
'God loves you' but forget to tell them that whom God

really loves He chastens. Joy becomes reduced to light-hearted banter. The result is that with suffering comes disillusionment and the feeling that somehow God has let us down. Our brothers and sisters in Russia, Eastern Europe, China, Vietnam and Kampuchea know better. Stripped of the props that undergird the privileges and riches of Western Christianity, they have rediscovered the 'fellowship of Christ's sufferings' as something to be known and not feared.

The Lord had to wait a number of years before Abraham could take a lesson of this kind. As with the disciples, the Lord had to say, 'I have much more to say to you, more than you can now bear' (John 16:12). There is an appropriate time for everything. Patience has to be developed. Faith has to be strengthened. God has eternity to fulfil His plans. Why should He hurry? We may be allowed to face depression now because God knew we could not take it earlier, and He may want to teach us from it and through it in a way that we could not learn without the darkness. Could Abraham have really appreciated what the slavery would mean, if he had never known the darkness? There are no quick and easy answers, even in the Christian life. We have great promises from God, but they are not lightly attained. Life is a serious business.

Suffering was not something Abraham wanted to know about, but something he needed to know about. And in learning about it Abraham was being let into some of the secrets of the universe. The kingdom would come, but only after the slavery. So Peter warned the suffering saints of his day not to wilt under their sorrows or look upon them as strange, and not to chafe under the puzzling delay in the coming of the kingdom (2 Peter 3:8,9). The kingdom would come, but only after the last person had come to repentance.

In the middle of the horror of his nightmare the Lord made clear to Abraham that he would 'go to your fathers in peace and be buried at a good old age'. He would not in fact see the fulfilment of his greatest hopes for his inheritance during this life. Other factors made that impossible. His faith and patience were being asked to take the long, the eternal view. For Abraham, the pioneer of faith, that was a very big step. He had come out from his land looking for an inheritance in a new one, and now he had to face the fact that the vision still lay a long way ahead beyond his lifetime. Sometimes the Lord has to bring us through days of darkness that our view might be stretched to take in eternity, where true fulfilment lies. We have so much more than Abraham to go on. We have the resurrection of the Lord to assure us that our labour is not in vain. Even though the Lord may not return in our lifetime, we have a hope already made more sure. Yet, in a measure, for all God's people there has to be that patience of the saints that sees beyond the immediate difficulties into the glories of eternity. But sometimes it takes suffering or depression to open our eyes to our true hope.

We may take encouragement, too, from the time when at last the fire of God did fall upon the sacrifice Abraham had so carefully laid out. 'When the sun had set and darkness had fallen,' when all was at its blackest, 'a smoking fire pot with a blazing torch appeared and passed between the pieces' (Genesis 15:17). God did seal His side of the covenant and gave to Abraham that fresh assurance for which he had been asking. The sacrifice was accepted and the promises guaranteed. The Word of the Lord of verse 9 was now matched by the fire of the Lord of verse 17. Similarly, we as Christians are aware that it was under the very shadow of the cross that the New Covenant was sealed 'in my blood', and each time we partake of the Lord's Supper we can receive fresh assurance that the promises of that covenant cannot be broken. We may face many a depression, but the Lord faced Gethsemane, and if Abraham could wait in patience for the consummation of his hopes, surely we can do the same.

10

Faith and home-made solutions

'Heaven helps those who help themselves.' At least that is the conclusion of one of Aesop's fables, and the belief of many people. We feel that we are not meant to sit around doing nothing when there are problems crying out for solution. In some cases this feeling is right and good. We can do something about the starvation and disease in our world, and only to pray about them is irresponsible. On the other hand, there are some situations where we can do nothing valuable and where God tells us to wait for His time. Most young people want to get married, and as the years go on become very anxious about it. Then they face the real temptation to act quickly and even desperately rather than wait for God's person to be brought into their lives. There are also times when we feel that God intends us to move in a certain direction, and yet we are bound by our circumstances to stay where we are for the time being. We get restless and look for a way out. On other occasions we may be faced with an acute anxiety about our health or that of a member of our family, our financial situation or our security. Here particularly it is hard to sit still and wait and the urge comes upon us at least to do something. A part of our education in the life of faith is to learn to wait in patience for God's own time for the fulfilment of His own promises, and to be prepared to do nothing active to relieve our feelings. In fact, if we do act we frequently complicate the situation unnecessarily and finish up even more frustrated than before. Abraham learnt this lesson the hard way.

The problem occurs when we have in our power the possibility of doing something that will accomplish our desire without our having to trust God for the fulfilment. So we manipulate our circumstances to get what we want. Already we have seen Abraham complaining to God that 'You have given me no children' (Genesis 15:3), but in chapter 16 he faces the possibility of a human way round the difficulty that will save waiting for God to give Sarah a child: and the suggestion came from Sarah herself. She said to him, 'The Lord has kept me from having children. Go, sleep with my maidservant; perhaps I can build a family through her' (Genesis 16:2). This was a perfectly normal solution in contemporary society for childless families, so that it was all the more easy for Abraham to agree to follow it. The sad thing is that Abraham decided to follow this course so soon after God had renewed His promise that He would provide a child naturally, and had confirmed His word with a remarkable experience.

Chapter 15 of Genesis leaves Abraham at the height of this experience, with the fire of the Lord sweeping down on his sacrifice, and the word of the Lord setting out in detail the peoples whom his descendants were to displace in taking over the land. But when we find the man of faith back home again in chapter 16, his wife is wrestling with the same problem over which he has just gained a remarkable victory and he comes down to earth with a bump. We are probably all familiar with the feeling of elation and well-being at the climax of a series of meetings or a conference and the sense of let-down that follows when we return to our daily lives and find the old problems still there. Things seem so different in the cold light of Monday morning. Abraham must have felt like that, for his faith, that had been able to rise above the setbacks of a sacrifice that seemed to go unnoticed, collapsed before his wife's desperation. The man who could dream dreams in the desert could not communicate those dreams to his partner in life. The man who was willing to wait for the fire to come down could not persuade his wife to wait any longer. We are no doubt too much aware of our own appalling inconsistencies to throw stones at Abraham. The heights of spiritual exaltation can so easily be followed by the depths of domestic disintegration. The disciples on the Mount of Transfiguration saw visions, only to find themselves powerless before a demon-possessed boy on the plain.

The enemy quickly whispers doubts into our minds concerning the reality of the first experience. How could it have been real if we fail so dismally so soon after it? The answer to that, of course, is that we are human beings with ordinary human reactions, and we are still sinful human beings. No spiritual victory today immunizes us against the most despicable failure tomorrow. We need as much grace every day at the end of our Christian lives as we did at the beginning. The trouble is that in the early days we knew that we needed it. After a spiritual 'high', we forget this and persuade ourselves that we can stand on our own. We cannot.

Another mistake we can so easily make, and that Abraham possibly made, is to assume that at home we can relax our spiritual defences. We forget that the Enemy takes no vacations and never relaxes. Home is part of the battleground. But just as we can so easily be less polite, less considerate, more selfish and quicker to react to slights when home with members of our own family, so we can lower our spiritual guard, and leave the Christian armour in the porch.

As Abraham returned home he probably thought that he had settled the question of childlessness for good. Now Sarah reopened the whole issue. I do not know what happened, but it is at least possible that Abraham had not shared his experience with his wife. Did it sound a little far-fetched in the cold light of day? Or was Abraham afraid to admit to his wife that he had questioned God in the first place? Was he now ashamed of that questioning? Maybe it was the other way round. Perhaps Abraham came home full of his experience and bursting to share it with his wife and she greeted his first words with some response like, 'You and your visions—what good are they to me? Remember, I have all the hard work to do around here. I can't afford to spend days in the desert dreaming. You brought us on this trip and away from our good home in Ur. Give me a son and I will listen to your dreams. Now let's get on. It's late enough as it is.'

The communication of our deepest feelings depends on a very delicate balance. In revealing them, we are revealing ourselves. We are afraid what we will look like in the cold light of day. We are afraid we will be rejected, crushed and discarded. So when we have gained enough courage to say something, the response we receive can settle for ever whether we will try communication at this level again. We half expect rejection anyway, so that if we receive it we retire in confusion, confirmed in a low self-image and hindered further from being and becoming the people we should be. This is particularly true for teenagers with their parents. When they run home, bursting to tell some news that to them has tremendous significance, and are met by cool indifference or a demand that they pick their clothes off the floor, something dies inside and a barrier to communication is erected that may take years to break down. Husbands and wives can do the same, building barriers of non-communication from the debris of past insensitive responses.

Whatever happened to Abraham, he had to face the problem of childlessness all over again, just as he felt he had received a clear answer. Some problems can be solved once and for all in a single decision or action, but others come back to us again and again in fresh guises and that is what makes them so hard to take. This time Sarah raised it. 'The Lord has kept me from having children' (Genesis 16:2). There was a note of complaint in the words she used. Instead of looking at the problem in positive faith, 'The Lord has promised me children,' she saw it in terms of negative obstacles, 'The Lord has kept me from . . .' The child withheld for God's glory, to develop their faith in accord with a loving educative purpose, was ascribed by Sarah to God's deliberate frustration of her desire, to a defect in God's action and character. Not the Lord has promised me, but the Lord has prevented me. Once we begin to suspect the Lord or think of Him unworthily, a root of bitterness can so easily spring up and become a potent source of trouble.

Convinced that God would not give her what she wanted, Sarah set about manipulating her circumstances to get it for herself. She could not control God, but she could command Hagar. By having a son by proxy through her, Sarah could force God's hand. We need to note carefully various aspects of her plan, for we can so easily do the same kind of thing.

Firstly, *she was acting under a heathen concept of God* in an attitude that expressed the essence of sin. The heathen idea of God is of a powerful being who, if we handle him aright, will give us what we want. The whole approach is based on self and selfish desire. God is not allowed to be God, directing, leading and providing in His love when and where He sees best for His purposes and our welfare. He is expected to submit to our will, not we to His. That is what happened at the Fall and has been going on ever since. We think we know the difference between good and evil in our case and God only needs to comply.

Secondly, given a problem that was eating away at her heart, *Sarah looked around for something to do*. Inactivity enervates. She could not bear the tension of going on waiting. She must do something. We are exactly the same. Quiet waiting is foreign to our nature. Instead of listening to the constant exhortations of Psalm 37 not to 'fret' ourselves because it only 'tends to evil' (verses 1, 7 and 8) and to 'commit your way to the Lord; trust in him and he will do this' (verse 5, and see also verses 3, 4, 7 and 11), we gnaw at our fingernails and cry out, 'If only I could *do* something!' But there are times when we can contribute nothing by our acts and, by bringing us to those times, the Lord teaches us to trust Him and to find Him real. By snatching at man-made answers we plunge ourselves deeper into the problem and rob ourselves of the opportunity to see Him work.

Thirdly, *Sarah may have acted out of a genuine desire to please someone she loved*. Perhaps she had a sense of guilt that it was all her fault that Abraham had no son. Maybe she saw herself as a failure of a wife and concluded that if God could not use her to give Abraham a son, He could at least use Hagar. A low self-image not only produces misery for the person concerned, but sometimes leads him or her to act wrongly and to set in train a vicious circle of guilt and failure that drags him or her down still further. Women are perhaps particularly open to this kind of temptation. Men generally do not so easily become burdened with a sense of guilt and failure, especially if the problem is a family one. But all of us are open to the peril of abandoning our principles to lay hold of something we feel we need and even that God intends us to have. Seeing no sign of its coming, we want to push a little ourselves.

And Abraham gave in. Faced with Sarah's pressure, he surrendered to it despite the fact that to do so was to act against his experience of life. As with history, so with experience. The one thing we learn from it is that we do not learn from it. Two women in one home asks for trouble. The Chinese people expressed this way back in their early history by expressing peace by a character which depicts one woman under one roof. Sarah was bound to feel worse once the baby was born. Hagar immediately became a rival in her own domestic preserve. Hagar had done for Abraham what his wife could not do. From now on she would constitute a continual threat. Sarah, in her intense desire and emotional involvement in seeking a son at any price, could not be expected to see into the future and know what would happen. But Abraham could. And for the good of Sarah, Hagar and his own domestic peace, he should have said, 'No.' One of the shortest words in the English language, this is one of the hardest to pronounce, especially to someone we love. Yet it is for want of the use of that word that many children are spoilt and lack a sense of security, men and women are

loaded with unbearable burdens of guilt, Christian
workers are too busy to pray and Christian resources are
consumed in ever-increasing quantities in unnecessary
conferences, meetings and a frantic bustling rat-race.
Abraham and Sarah had waited for God for ten long
years. Surely that was enough. Now they must *do*
something. We have waited two thousand years for God
to bring in His kingdom. Surely that is long enough.
Now we will do something and change the world on our
own. We have forgotten how to say, 'No.'

Abraham's success in his plan was his own undoing.
No sooner was the child born, than he had bitter family
strife on his hands. Success cut right across the promises
of God. This child was not the promised heir. No one
could see where he did fit. Contrived human answers are
no answers at all. Isaiah speaks of this. He refers to the
man who 'fears the Lord and obeys the word of his
servant' but who nevertheless 'walks in the dark, who
has no light'. He then speaks of such a man trusting in
the name of the Lord and relying upon his God. But in
contrast he goes on to address people who in such
darkness 'light fires and provide yourselves with flaming
torches' and concludes with the mournful judgement:
'This is what you shall receive from my hand: you will lie
down in torment' (Isaiah 50:10,11).

The torment came swiftly. As soon as Hagar was
pregnant, Sarah turned against everyone. She blamed
Abraham for Hagar's contempt of her and Hagar for
showing it, and she called on the Lord to do something
about it. The Lord had only come into her scheme when
she wanted vengeance; Hagar had been volunteered for
the job and Abraham had been told what to do; but she
blamed them all. Of course. Anyone with any
knowledge of human nature could have told her what

would happen. No other woman's baby could really satisfy Sarah and no servant girl could resist the temptation to put one across her barren mistress when she had conceived a son for the head of the house. It was all so predictable. The trouble is that under the extreme pressure of present desire, we are quite incapable of looking into the future rationally. The girl in love and longing to be married really cannot see that this man who may be her last chance will lead her a life of misery. Everyone else may, but she cannot until it is too late. The fellow who longs to have some money in his pocket really cannot see that this job which is so well-paid now is a blind alley and a miserable one at that. And when everything turns out as people around said it would, resentment is added to the sense of failure as the person hears in his mind, if not spoken outwardly, 'I told you so.'

The scheme ended in misery, misery for Sarah, for Abraham, for Hagar, for Ishmael, for Isaac and even down to this day for the Arab and the Israeli. In the Hebrew, verse 2 quotes Sarah as saying, 'It may be that I may be *built up* by her.' The destructive wars and terrorism of the Middle East today bear witness that destruction, not building, comes from human scheming contrary to the will of God. As in a spy story, we could add the famous words to man-made scheming: 'This will self-destruct in five seconds.' Some man-made schemes take a little longer but are no less sure in their result.

Just at this point Abraham made another mistake by again abdicating his leadership in the home. Instead of insisting that Sarah treat Hagar fairly and live with the consequences of their scheme, he threw all the weight of the problem on Sarah for decision and proclaimed the

dangerous principle: 'Your servant is in your hands. . . .
Do with her whatever you think best' (Genesis 16:6). In
the first place he should have refused the scheme, and
now he should have talked to Hagar himself about her
attitude. But he could not face it. So he left Sarah to
make a decision and he left Hagar at her mercy.
Moreover, he put out the false principle that power can
be used selfishly and authority can be exercised
arbitrarily.

He was right that Hagar was in Sarah's power. He
was wrong that she could do as she pleased. Power is a
sacred trust, not for selfish indulgence. Authority is right
and proper, but must not be abused. Much of the
modern rebellion against authority stems from its abuse.
The source of any authority ultimately lies in God and
without Him has no legitimate backing. But the
accompaniment to authority is responsibility and
accountability. Authority comes, not to enable us to do
'whatever we think best', but to enable us to use it for the
good of all concerned and with an awareness that the
One from whom we receive it will one day call us to
account.

The parents who use their God-given authority over
their children to compel unreasonable obedience so that
they themselves can do as they like are asking for
teenage rebellion. The whole history of industrial
relations is strewn with examples of employers who have
abused God-given authority to exploit employees and
expect them to comply and to live on unfair wages and
in poor conditions. No wonder trade unions now begin
negotiations on the basis that you cannot trust 'them',
and sometimes abuse their present power position to do
as they please. Power exercised to get what we want has
a way of coming back and hitting us hard. Misuse of

legitimate authority in the past has left us with a legacy
of mistrust, rebellion, obstinacy and chaos in state,
factory and home. Such things take years to overcome.

The whole story of Hagar's baby overflows with
errors. Yet they all stem from a reversion from the life of
faith. Sarah wanted to take her destiny and that of her
family out of the hands of God and into her own control;
and Abraham went along with it. How much harder to
wait and trust! And how much harder we find it to wait
for God's partner for our life, for His dealing with our
teenage children, for His solution to some knotty
problem, for His provision for a minister for a church!
But the life of faith has to be learned, and this is how we
learn it. The trouble is that, in our age, 'do-it-yourself'
has become such a habit that we find it doubly hard to
submit to the loving discipline of our heavenly Father.
Frantic action and fearful frustration come to us more
easily than faith.

11

Faith and fresh experience

We would hardly be normal people if we did not face periods in our Christian lives when nothing seems to be happening. We still read our Bibles and pray. We go to church, week in and week out. We live day by day in our usual routine, but somehow God does not seem as real as He did once. We are not conscious of anything that has gone particularly wrong and we know that the Lord is still there, but we wonder if anything is really taking place and where it will all end. Then, all of a sudden, and without any seeming reason for the change, we begin to discover new things about God, become more sensitive to what He wants from us and enter upon a whole new dimension of Christian living. We are not the first people to go through such times. Abraham went through them. Chapter 17 of Genesis describes one such period.

He was now ninety-nine years old, and that means that thirteen whole years had passed since his fatal involvement with Hagar and the birth of Ishmael. Nothing is recorded of those years. Presumably he carried on living as he had done before, and he continued worshipping the Lord as he moved from place to place. The promises of God were still with him, but they moved no nearer to their accomplishment as far as he could discern, even though every day was in itself an advance towards fulfilment. How do we explain such a time? Maybe the Lord had to teach Abraham patience and that his own rash act to obtain the end through his own means meant the postponing rather than the achieving of the ultimate end. Or possibly God simply waited for Abraham and Sarah to mature in life and faith to that point at which they could be entrusted with the child of promise. We cannot be dogmatic. What we do know is that God is never in a hurry, and he builds Christian lives through the slow process of daily maturing as much as in the more spectacular process of constant confrontation. Therefore a long period of seeming inactivity on His part does not necessarily mean that we have done something terrible to displease Him, or that He has stopped being gracious to us, but may simply mean that He is allowing us to mature step by step through the means of grace and the daily response of Christian discipleship.

The initiative remained with God, and it was He who broke the pattern by appearing to Abraham with a new realization of His own majesty and greatness. As we read Genesis 17 we find that all the talking is being done by the Lord and Abraham comes in at the level of obedience and action. We cannot tell God when He must come to us and what He must do for us. He is the Lord and we are His servants and when God really meets with us we find, as Abraham found here, that the first element of a fresh experience is *a new or renewed understanding who God is*. 'I am God Almighty,' El-Shaddai, the all-powerful, all-succouring God.

A new experience with God opens new avenues for our thinking. We see Him in a way that we did not see Him before. There are many names for God in the

Scriptures and they each contain some aspect of the being of God that conveys an idea of His character. We not only need to know what those names are and understand their meaning with our minds, but we need also to experience the truth that they contain in our own relationship with God. Elderly Abraham and barren Sarah needed to know that the God who had promised them a son was in fact all-mighty and able to fulfil His purpose even on the verge of Abraham's one-hundredth birthday. God knows exactly what reassurance and help we need and He is quite capable of moving in to provide it at the right time. As we come to experience the reality of His character in a new way, so our knowledge of Him grows. For our relationship to God is not totally different from other personal relationships. As they deepen, so our understanding of the other person grows and we learn new things about him and new aspects of his character that we did not know were there before. In our relationship with the Lord we need at times to see His holiness, at others His love; at one time we need to see His distance from us in morality, thought and action, at another His closeness to us in comfort, strength and encouragement. Because our age is so largely man-centred, Christians tend to spend too little time thinking on the nature of God, and less time in His presence. We do not therefore enjoy the closeness of the knowledge of God that Abraham possessed.

Along with the revelation of a new name of the Lord came a flood of reassurances of growth and fruitfulness. 'I will greatly increase your numbers.' 'I will make you very fruitful; I will make nations of you, and kings will come from you' (Genesis 17:2,6). After the thirteen years when it seemed as though God might have been inactive, He showered Abraham with promises to 'confirm my covenant', 'establish my covenant' and to give the land as an 'everlasting possession to you and your descendants after you' (Genesis 17:2,7,8). There was nothing startlingly new in any of these, but they revived the thrill of the early days and restored the excitement of what it means to walk with God. When we come to understand in experience an aspect of the character of God that has simply been a doctrine before, many other familiar truths come alive again, too, and our whole spiritual life receives a boost.

The greatest promise given to Abraham at that time is one that echoes down the pages of the Bible from Genesis to Revelation as the all-inclusive promise of God to His people. He said, 'I will establish my covenant as an everlasting covenant . . . to be your God and the God of your descendants after you.' We find the same basic promise in Revelation 21:3 where a loud voice from the throne of God declares, 'Now the dwelling of God is with men, and he will live with them. They will be his people, and God himself will be with them and be their God.' At this point Revelation adds nothing to Genesis. The promise to Abraham differed in no degree from the promise to every Christian, for we cannot possess more than God Himself. Here is the heart of the gospel. Salvation does not stop with the forgiveness of sins. That is but the first step that removes the fatal barrier to all the others. Our ultimate hope, assured to us through the cross of our Lord Jesus Christ and the gift of the Holy Spirit is that we might partake of the glory of God (Romans 5:2), or in the words of Peter, 'participate in the divine nature' (2 Peter 1:4). Such a goal provides infinite possibilities for growth and progress. How sad it is when Christians never move beyond the early stages of forgiveness and acceptance, but remain content to paddle in the shallows of a fathomless sea.

The second element in a fresh experience of God is often *a new appreciation of the purposes of God for the individual believer*. We have already seen the wider purposes of God for all His people in the intimate knowledge of God as their God, and in His adoption of them as His people. But God also came to Abraham and assured him of personal participation in the purposes of God by changing his name from Abram to Abraham (Genesis 17:5). Abram means the father of a people, but Abraham multiplies that idea to encompass a host of peoples, many nations. At the same time Sarah was not left out, as her name was changed from Sarai to Sarah, the latter name meaning 'princess'. The new name came to them both while there was no visible change in their circumstances. They still had no child. They were still the same people that they were the day before, but their new name put before them the promise of God and the potential for change. In the East names bear deep significance, and in the Bible names signify the intentions of God for that person rather than his or her achievement. Simon the shaky is told that he is Peter the firm; Jacob the schemer becomes Israel the prince with God. Just as God redeems us and then tells us to live as a redeemed people, so He calls us by new names and then tells us to live up to them. So Christians are 'set apart' or 'sanctified' in Christ and then called to be saints. We are made something, before we are called to be like that. The world demands that we prove ourselves first, and then maybe they will accept us, but God works the other way round, and the motivating power of His love is correspondingly higher. So a new experience of the Lord brings a new appreciation of His high purpose for us as people and we receive a new impetus to spend our lives living up to His expectations, in the strength that only he can supply.

We may take courage, too, from the Lord's changing of Sarah's name. She had been the one to suggest the scheme that would circumvent God's plan and in the light of what had happened she could have easily been feeling that she had ruined everything. Could God use her to accomplish His purposes now? He came to her and called her, not a failure, but a princess and confirmed to Abraham that 'I will bless her and will surely give you a son by her' (Genesis 17:16). The Lord does not hold grudges. Sometimes we can feel that one false step has cut us off from the deepest purposes of God. We even teach that if people do not respond to some particular teaching they may be found enjoying only God's 'second best'. Thankfully, I do not believe that is necessarily so. Peter denied his Lord, but became a leading apostle. Paul persecuted the church, but God showed him grace and he laboured more abundantly than the rest. Sarah had worked on her scheme, but she was still to become the mother of the child of promise. Certainly she had to live with the results of her scheming, results that she had to endure every day. We may have to do the same, but neither she nor we have to go through life with a constant burden of guilt for some past sin or mistake under the mistaken impression that God does not love us any more.

The effect of God's new revelation to Abraham was to throw him flat on his face. Twice in Genesis 17 we read that 'Abraham fell face down' (vv.3,17). For all his closeness to God and despite his being called the 'friend of God', Abraham never lost a consciousness of the distance that separates the Creator from the creature, mortal, finite, insignificant man. As God came to him afresh he learned to fall on his face in awe and adoration. We are not told in fact that this had taken place in the earlier appearances. Maybe it did, but certainly now the deeper revelation provoked the deeper reverence, and the closer we approach to God the more we sense His majesty and glory—majesty and glory that are not the less great for being associated, as in this passage, with His purposes of grace. When truly seen, the love and grace of God are as awe-inspiring as His holiness and greatness and wrath. We who live in the West today, with the strident voices of militant movements yelling for equal rights for all and in the process refusing any possibility of difference or excellence, find it hard to respect any authority, let alone experience a sense of awe. So when we come to worship we see no incongruity in telling God as we would our friend down the road, 'I appreciate You.' The thought that such an approach is near to blasphemy does not even begin to concern us, for we have lost our sense of distance and we are all on the same level together. In reacting against formality and dead ritual with freer forms of worship, we have to be careful lest a false familiarity destroys our understanding that God is, after all, God. Abraham knew the closeness of the Lord, but he also knew his place before Him.

We find one more strand in the threads that make up a fresh experience of God, and that is a *fresh understanding of what God requires*. Not only does God say to Abraham, 'I am God Almighty,' but also, 'Walk before me and be blameless' (Genesis 17:1). The Lord requires from His servant a walk in fellowship and in righteousness. Justification by faith is not intended as an excuse for low standards. In fact the standards are higher than before. What is different is the means of attaining them and the power to do it. Jesus said to His people, 'I tell you that unless your righteousness surpasses that of the Pharisees and the teachers of the law, you will certainly not enter the kingdom of heaven' (Matthew 5:20). There is no lowering of standards there. The difference in Christ is that we are clothed with the righteousness of Christ and then given the power of the Holy Spirit to live as He directs. Therefore, just as Abraham is told to 'walk before me and be blameless', so we are told, 'Live by the Spirit, and you will not gratify the desires of the sinful nature', and 'Since we live by the Spirit, let us keep in step with the Spirit' (Galatians 5:16,25). The Spirit Himself can then bring out in us the 'fruit of the Spirit': 'love, joy, peace, patience, kindness, goodness, faithfulness, gentleness and self-control. Against such things there is no law' (Galatians 5;22,23). Freedom in Christ is not absolute freedom to please ourselves, but freedom to be the dependent creatures God made us to be and freedom to escape the shackles that our selfishness, our contemporary world, and Satan himself impose upon us, forcing us to conform to one pattern. 'You were called to be free', says Paul in Galatians 5:13, 'But do not use your freedom to indulge the sinful nature; rather, serve one another in love.' Cutting the chains of self-centredness sets us free to serve God and our fellow men and women.

Every new understanding of the nature of God brings with it a new sense that God is also asking more from us, and it may well be that the Lord had to wait to reveal Himself more to Abraham until Abraham in his turn was ready to respond to the greater demands to be laid upon him. Sometimes we complain that God is keeping us waiting, when in fact it is we who are not ready and He is waiting for us to mature before He can trust us with new things. We do not grow up in a day, and just as in our physical lives we have to develop to a certain

point before we can enter upon some of life's
commitments with real understanding, so in our
spiritual lives we have to mature first. This also means
that we cannot respond to all of God's will in a moment
of time. Therefore we cannot possibly say with real
knowledge that we have given God everything. We may
have expressed ourselves as willing to do that, but we
cannot tell if we have given Him something until he asks
us for it. Then the test really comes. Jesus had to say to
His disciples right at the end of His earthly ministry, 'I
have much more to say to you, more than you can now
bear' (John 16:12). I feel therefore that we must be
careful in what we say to people in asking them to
dedicate their whole lives to the Lord, lest we imply that
once that has been done there will be no places in the
future when we will have to struggle with ourselves to
give God our full obedience on a particular point. The
life of faith is a walk, and to walk we have to put one foot
in front of the other unceasingly. Paul's exhortation, 'Be
filled with the Spirit' (Ephesians 5:18), commands not a
momentary surrender, however sincere, but a constant
open responsiveness to His promptings and daily
dependence on His power.

The Lord now asks Abraham for an obedience that
involves cutting into his own flesh and permanently
marking himself as belonging to God. Circumcision
cannot be reversed. 'You are to undergo circumcision,
and it will be the sign of the covenant between me and
you' (Genesis 17:11). There is to be no going back. The
New Testament equivalent is expressed in Colossians
2:11,12. 'In Him you were also circumcised, in the
putting off of the sinful nature, not with a circumcision
done by the hands of men but with the circumcision
done by Christ, having been buried with him in baptism

and raised with him through your faith in the power of God, who raised him from the dead.' The Christian believer is asked for a commitment that does not just involve cutting away a piece of flesh, but the renouncing of the whole sinful nature and the surrendering of the whole body to doing God's will. Jesus died for us on the cross and gave Himself wholly for us, and we are identified with Him in both the cross and the resurrection, so that we may live as those who have died to the old way of life and who belong totally to Him. So from our side the commitment required means much more than cutting something out of our physical body. Rather it means cutting out anything from our lives that prevents us being available for God to use. Abraham had to do the cutting in his case and that meant a discipline of himself to face the whole painful procedure. So we are told to 'put to death the misdeeds of the body', to 'count yourselves dead to sin but alive to God . . .' and that we must 'not let sin reign in your mortal body' (Romans 8:13; 6:11,12). We are enabled to cut out things that we could not deal with before, because we can now do it through the power of the Holy Spirit dwelling within us, but we still have to do it. No amount of praying will get us up in the morning. We have to put our own feet on the floor. We have to learn that walking the way of the cross cannot be done without discipline.

The result of the fresh experience of God that Abraham experienced in Genesis 17 was *a new excitement and wonderment at the promises of God to him.* Abraham fell down laughing as he said to himself, 'Will a son be born to a man a hundred years old? Will Sarah bear a child at the age of ninety?' (Genesis 17:17.) I feel that in this statement is a mixture of faith and incredulity, a combination of amazement and doubt. The thing seems too good to be true, and too far out to be possible. Eventually Abraham offered to settle for God's blessing on Ishmael. At least he was alive and there. But God never compromises on His purpose, so while He agreed to bless Ishmael and to make him fruitful and greatly increase his numbers, He went on, 'My covenant I will establish with Isaac, whom Sarah will bear to you by this time next year' (Genesis 17:20,21).

Maybe a part of Abraham's problem was that the Lord was promising to use normal means in an abnormal way. Perhaps he would have found the thought of the virgin birth less difficult to take than his being involved in a seemingly fruitless venture, trusting the Lord against all his experience to make it fruitful. We sometimes are more willing to ask for, and expect God to use, the outright miraculous than for Him to use normal means in an abnormal way. We may find it easier to pray for a miracle of healing without medicine than to ask God to use the medical means in a seemingly hopeless case. We have to remember that all means are God's means, and whether He uses them or not does not really make a difference. All healing is God's healing, whatever the instrument. Every conception and birth is as real a work of God as that of Isaac. What we need to do is not to lose the sense of wonderment from the special cases, but reintroduce that same sense of wonderment into the more usual ones.

In any event, God is not prepared to settle for anything but the best and He was not about to let Abraham decide His purposes for Him. Ishmael would have his part, but Isaac was the child of promise. And we cannot decide God's purposes for Him either. We can only fit in to those purposes. We cannot decide His plans for our children. We cannot even force our faith upon them. We can only trust them to Him. Abraham's plans for Ishmael had to be abandoned and the boy left in God's care.

So the man of faith entered into a fresh experience of the living God. He came to realize more deeply just what God was like and to appreciate His purposes for His people. He found a new realization of what God was asking from him and experienced a new amazement at the wonder of God's goodness and love. Only one thing remained for him to do. He had to put into practice the new requirement. Like a sensible person, he did not hesitate or wait. 'On that very day Abraham took his son Ishmael and all those born in his household or bought with his money, every male in his household, and circumcised them, as God had told him' (Genesis 17:23). Obedience gets no easier by delay. Monday morning is the best time to put into practice the lessons of Sunday's ministry. Revelation without implementation is like water poured out on the sand, trickling into uselessness. New experiences of God call us to action, and the sooner we do it the better.

12

Faith faces the impossible

People who live in a rat-race society are usually in a hurry. We rush from home to work, take a hasty snack at lunch-time and rush home at the end of the day, only to rush out again in the evening. We want everything done yesterday and delivery at once. Like children on a car journey we are always asking, 'How long will it be before we get there?' When we arrive, we want to know how long it will be before we go home. So we want to grow quickly in our spiritual lives and therefore invest in the multitude of 'How-to-in-six-easy-lessons' books that flood the market. We want to see the end from the beginning and the results as soon as we can. We even envy people like Abraham who lived at a time and place when it was possible just to be. Yet the God we serve is the same as Abraham's God and in no greater hurry now than He was then. He who is prepared to wait forty years for the light from one tiny speck in the night sky to reach us is not pushed for time.

We must therefore be prepared for God to take His time with us and to reveal His will for us at His own speed. That revelation may be very gradual. In Abraham's case, in Genesis 11:30 the story of Isaac began with a barren woman. In Genesis 12:7 the Lord appeared to Abraham and spoke of his offspring who would one day be given the land, but the description of the offspring was not elaborated. In Genesis 15:4, God made it clear that the son to be born would not be adopted but born naturally. In Genesis 17:16-19 the Lord confirmed that Sarah was to be the mother of the child despite her advancing years. Finally, in chapter 18:10 the promise culminated in a definite time, for the child was to be born 'this time next year'. Twenty-five years passed between the first announcement of offspring and the last communication of the exact timing.

The Lord often deals with us in ways like this. Rather than showing us a blueprint for our whole lives, He slowly reveals His plan step by step, unfolding ideas that at first were only dimly perceived and gradually leading on to the specifics and the details. I am sure that all of us who have walked the Christian way for a number of years can look back and see this process in our lives. I began by studying law and then received a call to the ministry. After experience in industry and then theological training, I was ordained some six years later. My interests had been centred in Africa from a missionary point of view, but the Lord gradually changed those interests over a number of years to centre them on East Asia. Another six years later, my wife and I felt we would be in England for the rest of our ministry, when the Lord stepped in again and took us to Malaysia. After a further six years we found ourselves in Singapore where our main ministry has been exercised. We had no idea at the start where we would finish up. We would probably have been horrified at the thought years earlier, but God has His way of preparing and changing us all, so that He can bring us to His place of appointment in His own good time. Looking back over twenty-seven years, we can see as Abraham could after twenty-five, that God had His plan from the start. If we had asked Him, 'How long will it be before we get there?' and been told twenty-seven years, we might well have despaired at the start. Our God is not in a hurry.

In some ways, the specific appointment of a time faced Abraham and Sarah with the real crunch as far as their faith was concerned. Could they really reckon on what God said when they looked at their own elderly state? The promise of descendants in their generality could be contemplated more easily than a definite idea that those two people were actually going to have a son in one year's time. Faith was facing the impossible.

The Lord was particularly gracious in the way in which he communicated the good news to Abraham. He did not come with a voice from heaven. He did not come in a vision of the night. The Lord who was one day to dwell among men in human form came to visit Abraham and Sarah in that very form. The manner of the appearance was particularly fitting when we compare the birth of Isaac with the birth of Jesus. Sarah's son came into the world through the normal process of birth, but with an abnormal conception, when humanly speaking Sarah was totally unable to become pregnant. Jesus was born through the normal process of birth but without the intervention of a human father and through an abnormal conception of another kind. Sarah was too old; Mary was a virgin. Sarah could not conceive because she was past it; but Mary because she had not yet come to the point of marriage. From Sarah came the earthly people of God; from Christ come the heavenly people of God. In speaking to Sarah, the Lord said, 'Is anything too hard for the Lord?' (Genesis 18:14). To Mary, the angel said, 'Nothing is impossible with God'

(Luke 1:37). In a measure, both these experiences form a kind of parabolic commentary on every human life, for human nature cannot produce any form of being by itself. We are as barren as Sarah and as incapable as Mary when it comes to producing life within ourselves. Only the Holy Spirit's implanting of a new nature within us can produce the spiritual life that we all need. We must be born again of the Spirit.

The Lord appeared at Abraham's door at a most unexpected time, when the master of the house was sitting at the door of his tent to take his siesta in 'the heat of the day' (Genesis 18:1). Anyone who has lived in a tropical situation will know that he needed it, and that that is not the usual time to go visiting. It is encouraging to know that the Lord may call on us at any time of the day or night. The New Testament quotes the incident as a challenge to be ready to give hospitality. By doing so, Abraham 'entertained angels without knowing it' (Hebrews 13:2). Why is it that visitors never arrive at a convenient time? Just as we have settled down for a relaxing evening after a busy and frustrating day, the doorbell rings and the callers come, assisted in our modern society by fast transport and telephone lines. The visitor does not have to move out of his own front room to come calling for an hour or so. If we really knew it was the Lord coming to call, we would gladly lay aside the evening, but it is some stranger calling out of the blue and wanting to take some of our time. In the parable of the sheep and goats, Jesus used these words: 'I was a stranger and you did not invite me in' (Matthew 25:43). We are probably less aware of angels than we ought to be in our day, but the Lord still goes calling in various guises that bring Him to our doorstep as really as He came to Abraham.

Unfortunately we are not usually the gracious hosts
and hostesses that Abraham and Sarah were that day.
Their manner of receiving their guests portrayed all the
marks that still distinguish Eastern hospitality and lift it
so far above our Western way of welcome. Nothing was
too good for the visitors, unknown as they were, and
whenever they had come. Abraham still described their
visit as a 'favour' to his humble home and implored
them not to move on elsewhere. He saw to their comforts
and urged them to rest while he got them something to
eat. And that meal was something! What he, with true
Eastern humility, describes as 'something to eat' turned
out to be a specially prepared and selected calf, cooked
with curds and milk in the best contemporary style. He
called himself their servant and stood aside as they ate,
and when all was over, he accompanied them on to the
road as they departed, in a custom that still pervades so
many Eastern cultures. Such lovely touches of concern
seem out of place in our time-and-motion orientated
society, and for us to adopt them as ours would be
artificial and self-conscious. Yet we may still learn that
guests do count and in them sometimes the Lord goes
calling on His people.

The news that Sarah was to have a son in the next
year came to Abraham in the course of conventional
discussion at the end of the meal. To express the wish
that their host and hostess might be blessed with an
addition to their family was a normal compliment often
expressed by guests. The world was not over-populated
at the time and no doubt infant mortality made a larger
number of children highly desirable. This time the
expression came not as a wish but as a promise: 'I will
surely return to you about this time next year, and
Sarah your wife will have a son' (Genesis 18:10). The
impossible faced them.

Sarah laughed to herself at the thought. 'After I am worn out and my master is old, will I now have this pleasure?' she queried (Genesis 18:12). The Hebrew expression she used can be variously translated, 'worn out, withered, ready to fall apart'. How could God use someone who was ready to fall apart? Many a person has asked that question about himself or herself. We feel ready to fall apart, and sometimes our lives seem to have fallen apart and it seems laughable that the Lord could possibly put us together again, let alone use us to produce something fruitful.

The Lord came back to Abraham, questioning Sarah's laughter and putting to him the unanswerable enquiry: 'Is anything too hard for the Lord?' (Genesis 18:14.) We could all subscribe to the truth that nothing is too hard for God. The problem comes when we face a concrete situation where that belief is put to the test, and too often we then begin to say, 'Surely in this case it is too late and too difficult. If something had happened earlier, or if this circumstance or that one were different, then I could expect God to work, but not now. I am falling apart.' God's words were at once a rebuke and an encouragement. Sarah could not face having denied the ability of the Lord, so she said that she had not laughed. If we were faced with some of our unbelief we would find it just as hard to confess. We would have to say that we can believe that God could give a child to elderly Sarah, but we cannot really believe that the tangled web of our own circumstances and problems really will yield to the power and purposes of God. We can believe that Jesus actually rose from the dead, but it is hard to believe that our lives can be resurrected from the morass into which we have wandered. We can believe that the Holy Spirit worked to bring thousands and thousands of people to

Christ in the time of the Acts, but we find it impossible to
expect Him to bring our neighbours or our family to
Him.

I am not suggesting that faith is blind optimism.
Sometimes faith is used as an excuse for expecting God
to do things he does not intend to do. Believing our
phantasies to be the purposes of God will not lead to
their accomplishment. God had made it very clear to
Abraham and Sarah over a long period of time that He
was going to do this thing for them. Therefore faith in
His promise was not the creation of their imagination,
but response to His revealed purpose. We need to be in
tune with God so that we may know His purposes, and
then we can seize His promise that nothing is too hard
for Him to accomplish. Anything less than this is little
more than the power of positive thinking. Faith is no
brazen optimism that calls God to perform
impossibilities that centre in the desire of the optimist,
but the humble confidence of the man or woman of God
who is able to discern His purposes and then to rest on
His power to accomplish them, whatever the indications
to the contrary. In such circumstances we can echo
Hudson Taylor's dictum that with God a task is first
impossible, then difficult, then done.

When it comes to facing our problems, however, we
know clearly from God's Word that He does intend to
bring us through them, even though that does not
necessarily mean in the way that we would like. He may
want to teach us through some constant pressure, and
use it to mould our characters in His own likeness. He
may allow us to proceed further down the path that
seems to lead to greater inability, just as He allowed
Sarah to get older and older year by year until the hope
of a family had shrunk to a speck. When, however, He
steps in with His Word of deliverance and blessing, we

can rest assured that that Word is no mockery of our dreams, but the plan of Him for whom nothing is too hard.

13

Faith learns to pray

'The mid-week prayer time at the church . . . is still conducted by fifty-three churches (out of ninety-two surveyed) in spite of the problem of commuting. But for these churches, attendance at the prayer meeting is small, even for large churches. The average attendance is only about twenty people.' So runs a Church Growth report on a group of North American churches, covering both the United States and Canada. A survey of churches in Britain might reveal much lower figures. I very much doubt if they would be higher. What has gone wrong with our prayer meetings? Do we not believe in prayer any more? Even large and flourishing churches have to admit that the special meeting for prayer draws the faithful few and no more. Yet if we are asked if we believe in prayer, and even in corporate prayer, we will say that we do. Almost without exception every revival within the church has begun in the hearts of those who have begun to pray. What is the problem today?

After Abraham had entertained angels without knowing it, and indeed after the Lord Himself had revealed His secrets to Abraham, he entered upon a time of deep intercession for the condemned cities of Sodom and Gomorrah. How did he learn to pray like that? The answer lies not in the technique he followed, but in the simple truth that *true intercession is based on real communion.* We tend to make intercession the primary part of our praying. We tend to see prayer as an opportunity to obtain for ourselves or for others something that we desire. So we rush into God's presence, pour out our requests and rush out again to the real business of living. We have forgotten that intercession depends upon intercourse. No one can pray for others who does not have a close relationship with the Lord first of all. We can, of course, go through the rituals of intercession because we feel as Christians we should, but that only makes matters worse. We then breed the 'shopping-list' mentality in prayer, passing from one thing to another in superficial mention. That in turn leads to long rambling prayers and long dead prayer meetings. Young people stay away in protest at what they see to be a meaningless exercise. So lack of life in our prayer meetings calls for a look at the depth and reality of our communion with the Lord.

Abraham was ready to intercede for the cities of the plain because he had just spent some considerable time in deep communion with the Lord, and it was perfectly natural to move from one thing to the other. He lingered in the presence of the Lord and the Lord began to reveal to him His own concern over Sodom. Their relationship was such that the Lord had said, 'Shall I hide from Abraham what I am about to do? Abraham will surely become a great and powerful nation, and all nations on earth will be blessed through him. For I have chosen him, so that he will direct his children and his household after him to keep the way of the Lord by doing what is right and just, so that the Lord will bring about for Abraham what He has promised him' (Genesis

18:18,19). The man who was to be the father of the
faithful needed to be allowed into God's counsels of
judgement as well as of blessing, and he also needed to
be able to share God's concern for a lost world and to
learn to share that concern in a ministry of intercession.
So, arising directly out of their existing relationship,
God told Abraham His plans and Abraham learnt to
pray.

Even so, Abraham did not rush into a torrent of
words. When the Lord had declared what He intended
to do, 'the men turned away and went towards Sodom,
but Abraham remained standing before the Lord'
(Genesis 18:22). He knew the situation now, but he still
waited, and only after a time did he begin to approach
the Lord in intercession. Silence before the Lord settles
the heart, gathers the thoughts and reminds us of Him to
whom we speak. The psalmist who was called upon to
'come and see the works of the Lord, the desolations he
has brought on the earth', was also told to 'be still, and
know that I am God' (Psalm 46:8,10). When we face
mighty movements in the destinies of men and women
that shake the earth to its foundations, time quietly
spent before the Lord restores our perspective and our
confidence, and loosens the tongues of intercession. We
sometimes fail to pray as we should because we spend no
time at all in quietness.

The principle of linking communion and prayer
emerges clearly in the New Testament. Abraham was
called 'the friend of God' to illustrate the close
relationship he had with God. Jesus spoke to His
disciples and said, 'I no longer call you servants, because
a servant does not know his master's business. Instead, I
have called you friends, for everything that I have
learned from my Father I have made known to you'

(John 15:15). Just as the friendship between the Lord and Abraham opened the channel of communication of God's secrets between them, so the Lord Jesus promised it will be for us. The words in John appear in the context of Jesus' teaching on the vine and the branches, and no clearer or more fundamental teaching exists on the relationship of constant communion that there needs to be between the believer and his Lord. In that same context, and arising directly out of it the Lord says, 'If you remain in me and my words remain in you, ask whatever you wish, and it will be given you' (John 15:7). The promise of answered intercession proceeds from the call to consistent communion. The deeper the one, the more real is the other; the shallower the one, the harder the other. The problem with our prayer meetings points to something much deeper that needs attention. After telling His disciples that He would treat them as friends, Jesus said to them, 'You did not choose me, but I chose you to go and bear fruit—fruit that will last. *Then* the Father will give you whatever you ask in my name' (John 15:16). Abiding and obedience lead to freedom in prayer.

Abraham also learnt at this time that intercession is based on two kinds of information. *He needed information about the needs of men and the deeds of God.* Already the angelic visitors and Abraham had looked down towards Sodom, but Abraham needed more to go on than that. He needed to know the needs of the people and that 'the outcry against Sodom and Gomorrah is so great and their sin so grievous' (Genesis 18:20). He also had to realize that God was going to do something about it and that He would go down and see if what they had done was as bad as the outcry. The needs of men called for intercession and the deeds of God called for urgency. We have plenty of information at our fingertips concerning the needs of men. Abraham could only look over two cities that day. We have the world on our breakfast table and wars in our sitting-room as the press and television spread the needs of men before us. Our problem is over-information rather than no information, for just as it is hard to pray when we know nothing, so is it hard to know for what to pray when we know too much. We can also become inured to the sight of mangled remains, war-torn streets, or endless lines of undernourished people scraping a survival in the queues of refugees. As for the deeds of God and the urgency of a world facing judgement, somehow that has not penetrated our thinking to move us to the urgency that the times require. When it comes to praying for the rest of the world, we can so easily be content to leave it to a slot in a Sunday service or to those who 'happen to be interested in that place'.

Abraham, the man of faith, turned information into intercession because he knew his God. He only knew one family in Sodom and Gomorrah, and maybe they were specially in his mind as he prayed, but he also shared God's concern for a lost world and turned it into prayer. Today more Communists than Christians have a global strategy and pay the cost to achieve their goals. But God's concern has not changed, and Christ's great commission still calls His church to a world-wide vision and concern that find their expression in prayer. We have the information.

When he did start to talk, *Abraham based his prayer on the character and justice of God* rather than on the needs of men. He was aware of those needs, but his ultimate concern was the glory of God, or in other words, that, when the day was done, God should be seen in a true light as the kind of Person He really is. The Lord is the Judge of all the earth. Surely such a Person must be seen to be absolutely just. Therefore it was unthinkable that God could destroy the righteous with the wicked. Even to suggest such a thing was a slander on God's character. So Abraham reasoned, and so he expressed himself in prayer: 'Far be it from you to do such a thing—to kill the righteous with the wicked, treating the righteous and the wicked alike. Far be it from you! Will not the Judge of all the earth do right?' (Genesis 18:25.) Abraham was more concerned for the integrity of the moral government of the universe than simply and only for the fate of men and women. He was right, for a universe governed by a capricious deity without regard for rules or justice would be a monstrosity. Upon the righteousness and glory of God and His own innermost consistency hangs any hope of an ordered universe where morality can exist. Abraham pleaded this basic consistency as the ground of his request. Prayer that is solidly grounded on the character and glory of God becomes powerful prayer. We so often begin at the wrong end.

We can see also that even at this stage of intimacy with the Lord, *Abraham never lost the consciousness that God is God and man is as nothing before Him.* He referred to himself as 'nothing but dust and ashes', and meant it. He said again, 'May the Lord not be angry, but let me speak,' and again, 'May the Lord not be angry, but let me speak just once more' (Genesis 18:27,30,32). He felt his smallness before the majesty of God, and his finite frailty before the Judge of all the earth. While we may live in a time when the way to God through our Lord Jesus Christ is open and free, we still need to remember our position. Peter reminds us, 'Since you call on a

Father who judges each man's work impartially, live your lives as strangers here in reverent fear' (1 Peter 1:17). The familiarity that enables us to cry, 'Abba, Father,' needs to be counterbalanced by the creature-Creator relationship. The warmth of the one does not exclude the awe of the other. Heaven is not a democracy.

On the other hand, *Abraham combined his sense of awe with a boldness in asking.* As he went on praying, he began to ask for more and more. The longer he stayed, the deeper he prayed. Nothing deepens prayer like praying, and praying that leads to an assurance of an answer received. Some people have suggested that if he had gone on longer he might have secured the sparing of the whole city for Lot's sake. However, when we reckon that Lot and his wife and daughters and their two respective fiancés made up six of the ten people required for the sparing of the city, I doubt if Abraham felt he should take it any further. In fact Lot's two future sons-in-law displayed a contempt for God's saving grace when it was revealed to them, thinking he was joking, so that the city had almost nothing to commend it. For the present discussion, however, we can learn the need to pray on and the value of praying on when God reveals a purpose to us. We do not have to be afraid to pray and to ask great things of God.

Here then was a man who learnt to pray. Yet interestingly this passage occurred comparatively late in the history of Abraham's life. No doubt he had prayed all the time he had believed, and his communion with the Lord grew in day-to-day communion with him. On the other hand, some kinds of praying call for a maturity that may need years to produce. One of the wonderful things about prayer is that the smallest child can use it and the oldest saint still has more to learn. We cannot start too soon.

The end of the account says this, 'When the Lord had finished speaking with Abraham, he left, and Abraham returned home' (Genesis 18:33). The Lord had done most of the speaking that day and when the man of faith went home he remembered more of God than he did of his own prayer. If our prayer meetings were like that, we would have no problem of falling numbers.

14

Faith finds fulfilment and performs a parable

'I would never have dreamed that it was possible.' So has spoken many a person when God has suddenly intervened in their life and turned it upside-down. Who would have thought that Chuck Colson, one of the chief men involved in Watergate, would eventually give his whole time to a prison ministry, because having met the Lord and served in prison himself he could not resist the desperate need for help there? Who would have thought that Voltaire's house would one day become the depot of the Bible Society after that noted atheist and opponent of the Bible had died? Who would have imagined that one of the hardest and most bitter of those involved in the Sharon Tate murder in the United States would have found herself turned round to become a witness for the Lord Jesus Christ? Who would have thought that grasping old Zacchaeus would be standing up there promising to repay the people he had swindled four times over? Who would have thought that Corrie Ten Boom could have survived the concentration camp to tramp the world for Christ? Such things have happened all the way down history and are still happening today.

Abraham and Sarah knew what it feels like to have the same joy of the fulfilment of God's promise to faith.

Genesis 21:1 expresses it in the economy of words for which the Bible is noteworthy: 'The Lord was gracious to Sarah as he had said, and the Lord did for Sarah what he had promised.' God came as He said, and God did what He promised; He always does. We should be able to put our name in the place of Sarah's, for God is still the same. We need never doubt His ability or willingness both to do what He says and to fulfil what he promises, and therefore we do not need to chafe under His delay. For God fulfilled His word to Abraham and Sarah 'at the very time God had promised him' (Genesis 21:2). Never early, never late, the Lord keeps to schedule, but His, not ours.

The happy couple named their new son 'Laughter', for joy and amazement at the miracle of an old man and a barren woman producing a child. Sarah in her joy burst out, 'Who would have said to Abraham that Sarah would nurse children? Yet I have born him a son in his old age' (Genesis 21:7). Many of us can echo Sarah's words, 'Who would have said . . .? And yet I have done it.' People bound by habits and sins, who have found new freedom, weak and ineffective people, who have found new power, disillusioned travellers through life, who have found new meaning—all marvel at God's fulfilling grace. The God in whom Abraham believed is described in Romans 4:17 as 'the God who gives life to the dead and calls things that are not as though they were'. Very often the rest of the world is unconscious of the miracles that surround them. No one in Canaan that day gave very much thought to the new baby in the Hebrew encampment. For the family of faith, however, there was much more to the birth than just a new baby. The glory of the faithful God shone through that home as they realized that when faith steps out on God's

promises it finds the solid rock beneath. And so today
the Lord delights to produce His works in the fellowship
of His people, using the 'nothings' of this world to
confound the power structures and to prove that real
strength comes not from us but from Him alone.

In the southern part of Thailand a child of
missionaries received serious head injuries in a collision
with a bus. Local surgeons feared to operate and the
parents were told to expect the worst and certainly to be
ready for a seriously handicapped child. A missionary
surgeon offered to take the risk of an operation and the
local doctors agreed to allow him to do so if the parents
consented. They did. Contact with one of the top brain
surgeons in Australia brought the child the best help
possible very quickly. Who would have said that that
girl would now be a perfectly normal person, not
handicapped in the least? But she is. In Kampuchea,
faithful missionaries of the Christian and Missionary
Alliance worked from 1926 to bring people to Christ,
and the total result by 1970 encompassed seven hundred
believers. Who would have said that four years later as
Phnom Penh fell, some ten times that number would
count themselves Christians and, even more, that
despite the miseries and tortures of the last few years,
twice that number again would be wanting to believe in
the poverty of the refugee camps. Who would have said
that the church in China and Russia today would be
stronger than when Communist governments came to
power? But God has done it. Perhaps it would be
beneficial to us if we stopped right at this point to ask
ourselves what we could put between those words, 'Who
would have said. . . .?' and 'Yet I have done it,' or 'yet it
has happened.'

Of course, Abraham and Sarah had to wait, and they waited a very long time. We must not minimize that. Sometimes the waiting seemed never-ending and, far from growing brighter every day, the prospect of any fulfilment receded with each passing year. The fulfilment of God's promises does not always take place in a gradual way. We would like to see a growing prospect of fulfilment dawning upon our horizon, but God at times moves in spurts, and the time preceding a spurt may look very discouraging. So we may pray for something that year by year appears to become more and more impossible. Then God steps in and it is done. Jesus in His own life did not see growing acceptance that finally resulted in everyone recognizing His lordship. Rather, His popularity peaked somewhere halfway through His ministry, rose again briefly at the entry into Jerusalem and then plummetted swiftly to the chasm of the cross. In the darkest hour Jesus expressed His confidence in all that was happening to Him as being in the will of God, by crying out, 'It is finished,' but spectators could have been forgiven for thinking that it was He who was finished. Nothing could have seemed more impossible than His being Lord of the universe at that point in time. Yet He rose from the grave and reigns in glory today. Who would have said it was possible? But it has been done, yet only at the right time and preceded by few hopeful signs.

Scripture warns us here against some of our human reasoning. For one thing, we can persuade ourselves that good planning and firm action will lead in the end to the achievement of our aims. Certainly we should think and plan, and obviously we must work, but the result will not necessarily be the obtaining of our ends. We may find ourselves faced with almost total failure

and fruitlessness and be tempted to reason either that we
were wrong to start in the first place, or that we have
gone terribly wrong on the way. We may find, as Jesus
found, people leaving us or criticizing us and leaving us
alone, and we may wonder if our original vision was a
right one. Other people may tell us to give up and invest
our lives and action in some more fruitful activity. Yet if
God has really called us and the job we are doing is in
His purposes, we may need to persevere and go on in the
most depressing of circumstances, until one day we see,
or those who come after us see, the accomplishment of the
vision. The people of Israel felt during the exile that they
might never see their land again. The iron might of
Babylon loomed unbreakably above them. Then in a
night Babylon collapsed and Cyrus king of Persia
'decided' on a policy of letting communities return to
their original homelands. The Israelis could hardly
believe it. 'When the Lord brought back the captives to
Zion, we were like men who dreamed. Our mouths were
filled with laughter, our tongues with songs of joy. Then
it was said among the nations, "The Lord has done great
things for them." The Lord has done great things for us,
and we are filled with joy' (Psalm 126:1-3). We cannot
therefore conclude that any situation is hopeless. Nor
can we say that if we follow certain methods or plans we
will necessarily see certain results. God is not at any
man's beck and call and He moves in wonderful ways to
perform His works. What we do know is that if
something is His work, it cannot fail in the end.

One cloud hovering on the horizon cast a shadow
over the joy of those days for Abraham and Sarah. A
thirteen-year-old boy shared the same home as the son
of promise. Naturally he felt that he had lost his place,
and he found it hard to conceal his resentment. Things

came to a head at a great feast to mark the weaning of Isaac. 'Sarah saw that the son whom Hagar the Egyptian had borne to Abraham was mocking' (Genesis 21:9). Was he despising this small bundle of flesh about whom the feasting centred? Was he saying to himself, 'Is this really the fulfilment of God's promise? What has he got that I do not have? I am the son of Abraham, too, and I am the first-born, and the stronger one. Why make all this fuss about Isaac?'

Sarah saw trouble and she saw red. With a woman's intuition she recognized that if Ishmael stayed around, Isaac could find himself bullied in his own home. So she said to Abraham, 'Get rid of that slave woman and her son, for that slave woman's son will never share in the inheritance with my son Isaac' (Genesis 21:10). To our thinking that probably seems unjust and harsh and rather selfish. We cannot, however, expect Sarah to share a New Testament ethical view of the matter, and we have to bear in mind that her behaviour found ready acceptance in her own culture. Not all our cultural behaviour is very Christian. Abraham felt her demand very keenly. Ishmael was his flesh and blood. For thirteen years they had been together and at one time Abraham had pleaded that Ishmael might fill the place of the promised son. But God stepped in and made it perfectly plain that whatever Sarah's motives were, the son who was the fruit of human scheming could never find a place alongside the product of God's promises. And thereby Abraham and Sarah performed a parable.

Paul develops this idea in Galatians 4:21-31. He says of the casting out of Ishmael, 'These things may be taken figuratively, for the women represent two covenants. One covenant is from Mount Sinai and bears children who are to be slaves: this is Hagar. Now Hagar stands for

Mount Sinai in Arabia and corresponds to the present city of Jerusalem, because she is in slavery with her children' (vv.24,25). In other words, Hagar and Ishmael may be taken to represent people who are under the law that came from Mount Sinai, and under the covenant formed there. This decreed that if Israel would keep the whole law, then she would be God's people. That in turn resulted in a form of slavery to rules, rules which no one could keep and which became increasingly burdensome because they only brought a sense of condemnation and failure. Ishmael as the son born from a human plan and effort stood for all human efforts to justify ourselves before God and to achieve a right relationship with Him by the keeping of laws. Contemporary Judaism in Paul's day acted and lived on this basis. Today multitudes of well-meaning sincere people do exactly the same, fondly believing that that is what Christianity is all about.

Paul then went on to say, 'But the Jerusalem that is above is free, and she is our mother' (Galatians 4:26) and also, 'Now, you, brothers, like Isaac, are children of promise' (v.29). The parallel to Isaac and Sarah is that group of people who have to admit that of themselves they have no power whatsoever to produce life within themselves, and no hope of gaining acceptance with God on the basis of anything that they can do. What they do, however, is to accept the promise of God made in the cross of our Lord Jesus Christ that if they repent of their sin and commit their lives in trust to Him who died for them, then God will invest them with His righteousness. From that point on they have complete acceptance with God, and are free from the depressing slavery of having to keep this and that law to try to gain acceptance.

The point Paul finally makes is that these two systems

are mutually antagonistic and one cannot survive alongside the other. We cannot have it both ways. He also makes clear that those who follow the second way are far from popular with those who follow the first. 'At that time the son born in the ordinary way persecuted the son born by the power of the Spirit. It is the same now' (Galatians 4:29). In the Galatian church there were those who still wanted to be tied to rules and regulations and to make acceptance dependent upon keeping them. But this was to negate the freedom and power of the gospel and to cast doubts on the power of the Holy Spirit to change people's lives, not by the threats and promises of punishments and rewards, but by the expulsive power of a new affection.

Human nature is still the same. We are incurably do-it-yourself. We find it next to impossible to say that we can contribute nothing to our salvation. Surely, we think, I can at least keep most of the laws and God will overlook the rest. So we struggle on to do our best and hope that the good deeds on the credit side of the ledger will eventually balance out the bad ones. We forget, of course, that no good deed has the slightest effect on any previous bad one, and we were really bound to do it, anyway. So we struggle with our pride. Then perhaps one day we see how foolish we are being, and, looking at the cross of our Lord Jesus Christ, realize that because He has done it all, including the cleansing of all that is past, we can find perfect acceptance in Him. We cast aside our own works and accept His work and confess,

'Nothing in my hand I bring,
Simply to Thy cross I cling,
Naked come to Thee for dress,
Helpless, look to Thee for grace,
Vile I to the fountain fly,
Wash me, Saviour, or I die.'

We cast out our old Ishmael spirit, the fruit of self-made effort, and we rest on the promise that as really as Sarah was given new life to bear a son, so the Spirit of God can create a new spiritual life in us. And then we must learn for the rest of our lives that these two systems of approaching and living before God cannot and will not mix. We never get beyond the stage when we are totally dependent on Him and His grace. For Jesus meant it when he said, 'Apart from me you can do nothing' (John 15:5).

So Hagar and Ishmael had to leave. But the Lord did take care of them. Abraham provided Hagar with some food and a skin of water and she wandered around the desert of Beersheba. When the food and drink were gone she yielded to depression, left the exhausted Ishmael some distance away from her and concluded that if he were going to die she did not want to watch it (Genesis 21:16). Like many of us when life's circumstances seem too much, she failed to see a well of water right close by and allowed her tears to obscure the solution on her doorstep. Once God had shown her the way out she gave Ishmael a drink and took new heart to find a new life-style in which Ishmael eventually excelled. The catastrophes of life do not have to be the end of everything. By God's grace they can be transformed into new and fruitful beginnings if we will let God take us by the hand, open our eyes, and enable us to see through our tears to the provision waiting for us.

15

Faith's final test

'I have worked in the church for many years and tried to serve God as best I can, and look where it has got me. How can God treat me like this? I cannot go to church again.' With words like these and a note of bitterness in her voice, a mother exposed her heart to a Christian worker. She had been a faithful member of the church for many years, but now her son in his early twenties had died in a motor accident and she was left with an aching heart and a bitter spirit. All that service of God did not seem to count for anything in the outworking of the divine providence. By her reckoning she had deserved better treatment. We can all understand her deep grief, and few of us would venture to accuse her of a wrong attitude, knowing the weakness of our own hearts, and yet she had not understood what the life of faith is all about. Perhaps in her sorrow she had forgotten that we do not relate to God on a bargain basis, that if we do so much, then He will respond with so much. He loves us too much for that kind of commercial relationship to satisfy His heart. He has something infinitely deeper in mind, and that something transcends even the most bitter of life's experiences and results in a union with Him that grows through the years and shines through the tears of earthly experiences.

We do, however, have to travel a fair way along
faith's pathway before we can be trusted with some of
the more perplexing of life's blows, without their
crippling us. When Genesis 22 opens, Abraham had
reached that point. Now he faced the supreme test of his
whole life, and he was ready for it. When he had left Ur
in response to God's Word and to His call to walk through
life with Him by faith, he had no real idea what it was
going to involve. If he had, he might never have started.
But any deep relationship grows slowly, as the people
concerned learn to trust each other and reveal more and
more of their deeper selves to each other. So, step by
step, the Lord led Abraham into closer and closer
communion with Himself, and with each step Abraham
learnt to trust God with something more that was
precious to him. In leaving Ur, he learnt to trust the
Lord with his friends, his safety, his business and his
material welfare. He did not know the land to which he
was going or what to expect when he arrived there. In
the quarrel with Lot, he learnt to trust God with the
choice of his inheritance. Then in the war of the kings he
ventured his life on the protecting power of God, and
when victory came to him he learnt to give in
thanksgiving. He then responded to God's call for a
sacrifice, and one that involved waiting and also
depression, coming through the darkness to a place of
greater confidence. In the covenant of circumcision,
Abraham committed himself at physical cost to the God
who was already committing Himself to the
relationship. Then, as the relationship deepened,
Abraham began to share the outlook of the great Lover
of the world and to trust God with the deepest desires of
his heart in prayer as he interceded for Sodom.
Eventually, at great personal cost, Abraham learnt to
trust God with his own son Ishmael as he left home to

find a new life in the wilderness.

We may look at these experiences in two ways. We may think how hard Abraham must have found it to be faced through his life with one thing after another that he had to surrender or which he found hard to obey. We may think God unfair to place such demands upon him. If we think like that, then we have not begun to see the infinite value of a personal relationship of love with the Creator of the universe. We may even be valuing things above people, or what we can get above what we can be. We have certainly missed out on the overflowing grace and love of God who condescended to call this man His friend. Alternatively we may think how amazing it is that God should come to a man like Abraham and progressively teach him, in situations that precluded any other explanation, that God is there, utterly loving and reliable and willing the good, and only the good, of His servant. We may think how wonderful Abraham must have found it to launch out time and again on a venture in which, if God were not there, he would have been seen to have been foolish in the extreme, only to find each time that God is absolutely faithful to all His promises.

Between these two outlooks lies the difference between a growing life of faith that is living and expanding and a stunted substitute that is still centred around self and what self can get from life. To some people today, Christianity means living exactly as we did before, but with joy and peace in our hearts, a smooth path ahead and heaven at the end. The radical nature of the change that a living trust in the crucified Lord brings has not dawned upon them. They have never known a situation where they were cast wholly upon God and nothing else, and therefore they have never known the joy of proving Him to be there and the growth in faith that such an experience provides. Careful not to expose themselves to any situation with which they might not be able to cope, they have never learnt the power of God to meet their need and the confidence that comes from finding Him faithful. When asked to do something beyond their present experience, they reply that they have never done it before, so they cannot do it now. Asked to think about giving a tenth of their income to God, they are afraid that they will not have enough on which to manage. Invited to stand up and share something with others, they say they would be too embarrassed. And so, unwilling to trust God for the small steps forward, they come to one of life's heavy blows without any experience to remember that will enable them to know that God will bring them through this one, too. Eventually, when faith refuses to launch out on the small things in confidence in the promise of God to sustain, it withers and dies. Static Christians soon become statistics, for a time on the nominal roll of church membership, and then too soon in the numbers of the lapsed. Yet at any time we may resolve to break this fatal slide into unbelief, find what God wants us to do, and obey Him in doing it, whatever we fear about the cost. Then life begins anew and the life of faith begins to take on a more exciting, if less safe, aspect.

Nor should we be surprised that the life of faith does not mean being carried on a bed of ease through life to glory. Jesus Himself said that, if a person was not willing to carry his or her cross and follow after Him, that person could not be His disciple. The concept of the Christian life as an easy respectable saunter through quiet paths corresponds neither with the New Testament nor with the effective periods of church history. Many young people turn away from

Christianity today, not because the demands are too great, but because so few demands are made that there seems nothing to live for, and certainly nothing to die for. If they could only realize the call Christ makes for absolute commitment in the adventure of knowing God, and the rewards available in terms of personal relationship with the Lord, they would find all the challenge they seek in the gospel.

Abraham, the prototype of the man of faith, went through a stiffer testing than most of us will ever face. Genesis 22 begins, 'Some time later God tested Abraham.' God said, 'Take your son, your only son Isaac, whom you love, and go to the region of Moriah. Sacrifice him there as a burnt offering on one of the mountains I will tell you about' (Genesis 22:2). Some people have rebelled at the very thought that the Lord should ask Abraham to offer up Isaac. Others have seen the command as an example of primitive religion in the evolution of Judaism. Both kinds of people have missed the point—that this was a test. Not all testing is wrong or unkind. We may test things for two reasons. One reason is to show how bad they are. The other reason is to show how good they are. When the car showroom invites me to test drive their latest model, they are not expecting me to come back saying how terrible it is, but hoping that I will see that it is so good that I will buy it. They have every confidence in the model, so they invite me to put it to the test. When, however, I have a machine that has persistently gone wrong ever since I bought it and I take it back to the dealer and ask him to test it, I do so to show him just how bad it is, in the hope that he will see it, too, and give me a new one. The Lord does not put us men to the test to demonstrate how bad we are, but to show how effective His work has been in us. He does it from a good motive, expecting us to pass the test and to gain confidence from doing so. And He knows just how much we can take. Often the prototype model goes through stiffer testing than anything that the ordinary kind will be expected to take. Maybe Abraham was a prototype in this way, too. He certainly demonstrated to all generations that the life of faith is real and works, and that any man or woman who responds to the Lord's call to walk with Him may be assured that He will bring His work in that person to a successful conclusion.

Abraham was drawing near the end of his life and growth in discipleship, and God felt able to apply to him the supreme test of all. Did he really love God more than anything, more than any of His gifts, more even than the fruit of His promises? He was saying something like this, 'Abraham, do you love Me or My gifts? Did you trust Me because I am God, or because you wanted a child? I want you to love Me and worship me and obey Me for Myself, because of who I am. Give Me back the fruit of My promises. Give Me your son, whom you love so much. Let there be nothing between us but the personal relationship, I and you. Between God and man, Abraham, this relationship can be very close, but it is still the relationship of Creator and creature. So give Me your son, your only son, whom you love.'

Abraham's immediate response indicates clearly that God for him was no creation of man's imagination. He was the one great Reality, the God who is there, the One he had learned to trust through many a smaller test. Abraham showed that his faith was not faith in faith, nor the reflection of the feelings of others in a believing community, but active trust in a living Lord who had spoken to him in specific terms. Put to the test in the darkest day, his faith shone the more brightly. Because

God for him was real, he did not crumple in front of the test.

In one sense Abraham had come full circle. His faith at this point echoed that first step of faith he had taken in leaving Ur. Then it had been the first faltering step of a new beginning. Now it was the confident strong step of mature conviction, but the basic elements were the same. In the first place God called him to go 'to the land I will show you' (Genesis 12:1). Now God told him to offer Isaac 'on one of the mountains I will tell you about' (Genesis 22:2). In neither case did he know exactly where he would finish up, but in both cases he trusted the One who gave the word. Abraham was moving to his culminating appointment with God.

Abraham obeyed at once. 'Early the next morning Abraham got up and saddled his donkey. He took with him two of his servants and his son Isaac. When he had cut enough wood for the burnt offering, he set out for the place God had told him about' (Genesis 22:3). Instant obedience eliminates second thoughts. Some things must be done at once or they will not be done at all. As far as we know Abraham said nothing to Sarah, and this time he was right. Some things cannot be shared even with our nearest and dearest. To have told Sarah at this point would have been to load her with an unnecessary burden of anxiety, and to invite a protest at obedience that would have been next to impossible to resist. Some roads must be walked alone.

For three days he trod his Via Dolorosa away from the place of family unity and safety to the place of suffering, death and heartache. There a sword was to pierce his own soul as really as the knife must pierce his son's body. For three days Isaac was as dead to him. Yet still he believed. When he left his men at the end of the road, he said to them, 'We will worship and then *we will come back to you*' (Genesis 22:5). Deliverance or resurrection made no difference. One must surely happen for, by now, Abraham knew, not just the promises of God, but the God of the promises. If God was asking him to sacrifice the son of promise, then God would be responsible for bringing him back to life again.

For three days father and son travelled together with the servants. Then 'Abraham took the wood for the burnt offering and placed it on his son Isaac, and he himself carried the fire and the knife' (Genesis 22:6). Then 'the two of them went on together', for at this point no one else could accompany them. What faced them had to be faced alone. Isaac asked the inevitable question: 'The fire and wood are here, but where is the lamb for a burnt offering?' (v.7.) Abraham's faith shone clear as he answered, 'God himself will provide the lamb for the burnt offering, my son' (v.8). Then the Genesis account significantly repeats the pregnant sentence: 'And the two of them went on together' (v.8). Isaac must have been a teenager by this time. Had he guessed what was in his father's mind, and was he ready to go along with it? Abraham at his age would have been hard put to it to bind Isaac and lay him on the altar if the young man had resisted him. We read of no struggle or protest.

All the time that Abraham was preparing the last grim ingredients of the tragedy, God said nothing. 'Abraham built an altar there and arranged the wood on it. He bound his son Isaac and laid him on the altar, on top of the wood. Then he reached out his hand and took the knife to slay his son' (vv.9,10). Then, and not until then, the Lord intervened. He had no intention of allowing Abraham to kill his son, but He did want to know how far he was prepared to go, not just in verbal professions of obedience, but in sacrificial acts. Now He knew. God was first in Abraham's heart and trust, and not even Isaac could usurp that primacy.

Abraham had told Isaac that God would provide Himself a lamb for the burnt offering, and provide the lamb He did. There on the mountain struggled a ram caught by its horns, ready to be taken and to be offered in substitution for the son of promise. We may still wonder why God had to go to such lengths to test His servant's faith, but the reason for the test becomes clearer when we think of the parallel experience, when God was the Father, and the Lamb was His own Son being offered up on a hill called Calvary. On that occasion the Son really died and the answer came, not through deliverance, but through resurrection. The victim was both Son and Lamb, substituting for the sinners of the world and dying for their sins.

The parallels are remarkable. Although Isaac carried the wood, Abraham carried the fire and the knife. Jesus carried the cross, but the Father as really carried the final burden of the death of His Son. Jesus willingly endured the cross, but He did not kill Himself. 'We considered him stricken by God, smitten by him, and afflicted. But he was pierced for our transgressions, he was crushed for our iniquities: the punishment that brought us peace was upon him, and by his wounds we are healed' (Isaiah 53:4,5). 'Yet it was the Lord's will to crush him and cause him to suffer, and though the Lord makes his life a guilt offering, he will see his offspring and prolong his days, and the will of the Lord will prosper in his hand' (Isaiah 53:10). We must never present the cross as though the Father were not actively involved in it. We must never suggest that Jesus the loving Son was dying to appease an angry Father God and thereby

trying to make Him love us. As really as Abraham and
Isaac went on together, so the heavenly Father and Son
went together to face the ultimate sacrifice of the cross.
Far from Christ dying on His own and separate from the
active involvement of the Father, we read that 'God was
reconciling the world to himself in Christ, not counting
men's sins against them' (2 Corinthians 5:19).

Just as God spoke to Abraham of a land at the
beginning of his walk of faith, and led him to a mountain
of sacrifice at the end, so the cross was inherent in the
coming of Christ to this earth. Calvary revealed the
purpose of Bethlehem and sealed the final
demonstration of the love of God to the human race.
What more could Abraham give in his love for God?
What more could God give in His love for men, than
what He gave when He 'gave his one and only Son, that
whoever believes in him shall not perish but have
eternal life'? (John 3:16.) When God asked Abraham to
give Him his all, He was not asking anything He Himself
was not prepared to give. But what is the little we have,
compared with the 'all' that is His? And here lies the
answer to the woman's question with which this chapter
began. We cannot, and never could, merit more than
God has already given us, because He has given His all
on Calvary. He may ask us to yield to Him something
precious to us, whether it be goods or money or loved
ones, but the dearest of these is as nothing compared to
His sacrifice already made and demonstrated. So we
cannot and must not doubt His love to us.

In the cross, God is speaking to us and saying
something like this: 'My child, I am asking you to love
Me first, and more than anything or anyone. I ask you to
love Me with all your heart and strength and soul and
mind. For this is exactly the kind of love with which I

love you. I have gone to the place appointed. I have gone up the mountain with My Son. He carried the cross, but I carried the knife, and I bound Him there and smote Him there, the Lamb of God that takes away the sin of the world. I love you like that. I am not asking from you anything I have not given Myself. My son, My daughter, give Me your heart. If I love you like that, can you not surrender those few worthless toys that you cling on to so much? If I love you like that, can you not persevere in that work for Me, continue to nurse that person for Me, or give over that friendship? I gave you My Son, may I not ask for the best years of your life on earth? Can I not take your son for My service across the world? Am I really asking too much?'

'Abraham returned to his servants, and they set off together for Beersheba' and Isaac was with them (Genesis 22:19). He returned with all the promises of God renewed, reiterated, confirmed, signed, sealed and delivered (Genesis 22:15-18). Nothing now could stand between Abraham and all that God had for him and for his descendants. We have the promises of God similarly visibly confirmed for us in the resurrection and ascension of our Lord Jesus Christ and we can say boldly, 'He who did not spare his own Son, but gave him up for us all—how will he not also, along with him, graciously give us all things?' (Romans 8:32.) With the resurrection behind us we know that nothing in heaven and earth can stand between the purposes of God and His people. Everything is assured.

16

Faith looks for a country

Normally realistic people in a down-to-earth age
strangely refuse to discuss the one great reality of life:
death and all that lies beyond. We can talk about
politics or abortion, women's liberation or Communism,
the economy or health, but death is too hot to handle
and too embarrassing to bring up. To consider for how
much to insure your life is good sensible preparation in
our scale of values; to think about how to prepare for
death and its sequel is morbid. So we hide the subject
behind an embarrassed silence that makes the Victorian
lack of openness about sex seem positively brazen, and
we hope that death will go away.

Just at this point, where brave humanistic philosophy
abandons its devotees to despair, faith shines with even
greater splendour and boldly looks, not only at death,
but far beyond it, into a new realm of ever-increasing
glory. So when we leave Abraham near the end of his
life, standing by a grave, we need not envision an
anticlimax to all that has gone before. When we look at
his surrounding circumstances, we might wonder if the
life of faith was really worth it. Sarah had died.
Abraham was old. All he possessed in the 'promised
land' was a field and a cave. The cave he had bought for
a grave, and he had paid a good price even for that

(Genesis 23). He had no estate in the land that was to become his, and he only had the one son of the promised line, with as yet no grandchildren. Yet Abraham was not down-hearted or despairing—far from it. Having seen the power of God to deliver Isaac from the jaws of death, Abraham had no doubt about God's ability to raise himself from the dead and to fulfil all His promises to him in His own good time. Faith could see beyond the veil that cut the future from his earthly sight, and was content to wait.

The grave by which Abraham stood was different from so many graves in the world. So many people slave and toil for security and riches all their lives, only to find in the end that all they really possess is a plot of ground six feet by three, and with no hope of anything more. For Abraham, as for all believers, the grave was like the cupboard in C.S. Lewis's Narnia stories, a cupboard that looked like any ordinary one with no way out, but which in fact contained a doorway to a whole new and exciting world.

The first time I expounded the life of Abraham at a conference, I was about to speak to the meeting when the telephone rang. The message I was going to give centred round the offering of Isaac and the death of Sarah, and the message that came over the wires that day brought news of the death of one of our fellow workers in a road accident just a few miles away. He was a young man with a wife and three children, and our hearts were sad. But as we turned to the Word of God together, we realized that He was turning our thoughts to the only real answer to the question posed by death, the answer contained in a picture in the restoration of Isaac to Abraham, and in practical reality in the resurrection and ascension of our Lord Jesus Christ.

Death is not the final word, for in Christ life extends beyond the grave and on into the farthest reaches of eternity, where we look for a new heaven and a new earth in which righteousness makes its home.

And so it is written of all God's people from Abraham's day to the end of time: 'All these people were still living by faith when they died. They did not receive the things promised; they only saw them and welcomed them from a distance. And they admitted that they were aliens and strangers on earth. People who say such things show that they are looking for a country of their own. If they had been thinking of the country they had left, they would have had opportunity to return. Instead, they were longing for a better country—a heavenly one. Therefore God is not ashamed to be called their God, for He has prepared a city for them' (Hebrews 11:13-16).

'These were all commended for their faith, yet none of them received what had been promised. God had planned something better for us so that only together with us would they be made perfect. Therefore, since we are surrounded by such a great cloud of witnesses, let us throw off everything that hinders and the sin that so easily entangles, and let us run with perseverance the race marked out for us. Let us fix our eyes on Jesus . . .' (Hebrews 11:39-12:2).

In the end faith's eyesight is seen to be more penetrating than the myopic vision that perceives only the temporal and the material. We may have to wait longer than others for our inheritance, but then we have all the time in the world—and beyond it. We can afford to be patient. We are empowered by faith.